Products and Plans for

UNIVERSAL HOMES

Over 1,700 Products from over 450 Manufacturers
Plus, 51 Plans for Universal Homes

The Editors of Home Planners
In Cooperation with The Center For Universal Design
and
The Philip Stephen Companies, Inc.

HOME PLANNERS, LLC
Wholly owned by Hanley-Wood, LLC
Tucson, Arizona

Designing for the 21st Century II

An International Conference on Universal Design

The *Designing for the 21st Conference* on Universal Design is a biennial conference that showcases state of the art universal design solutions and worldwide innovations in environments, products and information technology. It offers forums that consider universal design in design education and the larger context of social justice, sustainable development and successful business practices. The biennial event also features an exhibit hall, a bookstore and a media center. Please call 617-695-1225v/tty for the upcoming conference dates and location.

Conference Sponsors

Adaptive Environments
374 Congress Street, Suite 301
Boston, MA 02210, USA
617-695-1225 v/tty   fax 617-482-8099
21stcentury@adaptenv.org
www.adaptenv.org

Center for Universal Design
School of Design
North Carolina State University
Raleigh, North Carolina, USA

AdaptZ.com
When Life Changes...
www.adaptz.com
info@adaptz.com

Dedication

Ronald L. Mace, FAIA (1941-1998)

Ronald L. Mace, FAIA, founder and program director of The Center for Universal Design, was an extraordinary and visionary man. Ron taught those around him to resist the status quo and not accept "good enough." He understood that for all members of society to grow and develop, they must be able to participate with dignity and ease in all society has to offer. Ron believed that all people have the right to live their daily lives unhindered by their environment. His pioneering work in accessible housing was at the forefront of universal design, for Ron recognized that we are not disabled by accident or illness, but rather by our surroundings. As a designer, Ron practiced what he believed, making the world a little better place for everyone. As a teacher, he shared his ideas with others so that they would understand the spectrum of human conditions and build a better world for all. And as a leader, Ron accepted challenges and risks and moved ahead where others saw barriers. Today, Ron's work is being carried throughout the world. This book was one of Ron's last projects. He would be very pleased to know that many others will now benefit from his vision of more universal design in housing.

Universal design is the process of designing products and environments that are usable, to the greatest extent possible, by everyone regardless of their age or ability.

–Ron Mace

Acknowledgements

The Center for Universal Design
The Center for Universal Design, in the School of Design at North Carolina State University, is a national research, information and technical assistance center that evaluates, develops and promotes accessible and universal design in buildings and related products. Their mission is based on the belief that the built environment and products should be usable, to the greatest extent possible, by everyone, regardless of their age or ability. The Center also collaborates with businesses and industry on the development and evaluation of design solutions and marketing strategies. Major funding for the Center is provided by the U.S. Department of Education, National Institute on Disability and Rehabilitation Research.

The Philip Stephen Companies
The Philip Stephen Companies (PSC) is a design and development firm in St. Paul, Minn., recognized internationally for its work creating universal design housing and housing strategies which promote aging in place. PSC has developed universal design product line and promotional materials for numerous individuals, several national firms and their own projects in South Carolina where PSC is an active, licensed builder.

PSC was founded in 1987 by its President, Philip S. Dommer. Mr. Dommer is a 1985 graduate of the University of Minnesota with a specialized degree in housing and aging. He is a frequent speaker and instructor on the topic of active adult housing and is a Trustee for The National Council of Senior Housing of the NAHB. In 1997 he received the National Building Innovation in Home Ownership Award for his work developing affordable universal design homes for Native American elders and Habitat for Humanity.

Feature House see page 10.

Published by Home Planners, LLC, wholly owned by
Hanley-Wood, LLC, in cooperation with
The Center for Universal Design and
The Philip Stephen Companies, Inc.

Home Planners Editorial and Corporate Offices:
3275 West Ina Road, Suite 110
Tucson, Arizona 85741

Distribution Center:
29333 Lorie Lane
Wixom, Michigan 48393

Rickard D. Bailey, CEO and Publisher
Cindy Coatsworth Lewis, Director of Publications
Paulette Mulvin, Special Projects & Acquisitions Editor
Kathleen M. Hart, Project Consultant
Jan Prideaux, Executive Editor
Sara Lisa-Rappaport, Production Coordinator
Paul Fitzgerald, Senior Graphic Designer
Victoria M. Frank, Supervisor, Data Acquisition
Brenda McClary, Publications Assistant

First Printing: January 2000

10 9 8 7 6 5 4 3 2 1

Contents

Printed in the United States of America

Library of Congress Catalog Card Number: 99-72939

ISBN: 1-881955-65-6

*On the cover: This dramatic design is just one fine example of the versatility and
appeal of universal design. For more photos, floor plans and a description of the
home, see pages 10-13.
Photo by Bob Greenspan.*

Back cover photo by Bob Greenspan.

Nature created bacteria, mold, and mildew for specific purposes. None of which include bathing.

In the beginning, bacteria, mold, and mildew thrived in warm, moist climates. Like bathtubs. But now that Aqua Glass gelcoat tubs and showers have built-in Microban® antibacterial protection, it's a whole different story. Microban® inhibits the growth of bacteria, mold, and mildew that cause odors and stains, so Aqua Glass bathing fixtures are much easier to keep clean. Microban® is also engineered to last the life of the unit. It's everything your customers have been clamoring for. So when you install an Aqua Glass tub or shower in the home you build for them, they'll marvel at your creation. **Call 1-901-632-2501 or visit www.aquaglass.com.**

A Masco Company

AQUA GLASS®

With built-in Microban® antibacterial protection.

◈ Microban®
antibacterial protection

Pure Indulgence.™

Introduction

By Laurence H. Trachtman,
Executive Director, The Center for Universal Design

It is important to understand the basis of universal design, because, as the name indicates, it is not only for homeowners with disabilities or who are older, but also for a "universe" of people. Universal design is a design concept that recognizes, respects, values and attempts to accommodate the broadest possible spectrum of human ability in the design of all products and environments. This design philosophy helps eliminate the need for special features or adaptations that can be stigmatizing, embarrassing, different-looking and costly. Universal design is important to everyone, as we all, at some point in our lives, are likely to experience limitations due to age, illness or injury.

When well implemented, universal design is virtually invisible, safe and physically and emotionally accessible to most users. In simple terms, universal design is user-based "good design." It might be called "more inclusive user-based design" because it includes the abilities and needs of the widest range of people.

The Need for More Universal Design

Significant changes in today's society suggest that a design approach to make products and environments more universally usable is necessary. Dramatic declines in death rates associated with a variety of illnesses, injuries and age-related conditions have enabled an unprecedented number of people to live longer and more independently. In the U.S., people age 65 and older already number 34 million, a figure that is expected to double by the year 2030. But while statistics can be informative, designing for children, older people and people with disabilities is not thinking about separate groups of users but rather focusing on the spectrum of human-environment interaction.

Changes in who we are, what we can do and where we live require a world that is more accommodating to variances in mobility, vision, hearing, thinking and manual dexterity. All aspects of the home environment, including layout and products, will have to be redesigned as our needs change with age. In fact, the magnitude of the population shift suggests that it would make more sense to design products and environments for everyone rather than creating different designs for certain individuals. This insight underlies the movement toward universal design.

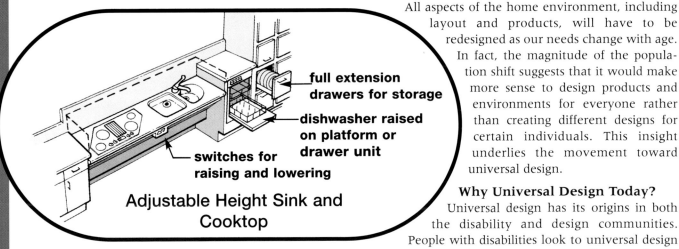

full extension drawers for storage

dishwasher raised on platform or drawer unit

switches for raising and lowering

Adjustable Height Sink and Cooktop

Why Universal Design Today?

Universal design has its origins in both the disability and design communities. People with disabilities look to universal design to increase the accessibility and usability of the built environment, as well as to enhance opportunities for participation and social integration in everyday life. At the same time, universal design has found proponents among designers and social scientists who see it as a means to achieve a wider definition of good design based on its responsiveness to the needs of users.

Universal design does not carry the connotations of the terms "barrier free" or "accessible" design, which can be required by laws and for which prescriptive standards can be made enforceable. There are no mandated standards or specifications that prescribe uni-

Easy-To-See™ thermostats keep you in control of your comfort

Comfort made easy

Honeywell's Easy-To-See thermostats are specially designed for anyone with decreased vision, blindness, or limited hand strength. They keep you in control of your comfort by making it easier to adjust your thermostat.

High-contrast markings and a low-glare design make it easier to see the current temperature setting. The temperature setting scale and switch markings are raised, for easy recognition by sight or by touch.

Temperature adjustments are easier thanks to a large, grippable temperature-setting dial or lever, and click-detents that provide audible and tactile feedback for every two degrees of movement.

The large-print owner's guide is easy to read. There's even an optional Braille owner's guide available (for a free copy call Honeywell at **1-800-345-6770, ext. 7175**.)

Easy-To-See thermostats are available for low voltage conventional or heat pump systems.

T87F Easy-To-See™ Round® Thermostat

Large-print decals and enlarged switch markings make it easier to select your settings.

Grippable, ribbed temperature dial makes setting the desired temperature easier. A click is heard, and indent felt, for every two degrees of movement.

Enlarged, raised numerals at 50, 60, 70 and 80 °F marks are easy to recognize by sight or by touch.

Easy-To-Use™ Accessory

A snap-on Easy-To-Use Accessory (available for all Easy-To-See Round® Thermostats) aids those with limited hand or wrist strength due to arthritis, multiple sclerosis, polio, spinal cord injuries, or other causes. It doubles the grippable area of the temperature adjustment dial, allowing users to easily brush or roll the dial to the desired temperature setting.

MODEL	COLOR	REMARKS
T87F3467	Gold	For heating, cooling or heating/cooling.
T87F5199	Premier White	For heating, cooling or heating/cooling.
TS86A1421	Gold	For 250/500 or 750 millivolt gas systems.
221886A	Clear	Easy-to-Use accessory snaps onto the temperature dial.
T841A1696	Taupe	Heat pumps with manual heat/cool changeover.

Your heating and cooling contractor will help you select the appropriate model for your equipment.

For additional information about Easy-To-See™ thermostats, or information describing other Honeywell products for people with special needs, call 1-800-345-6770, ext. 7175

Honeywell
Your Home Expert

www.honeywell.com/yourhome

Honeywell

versal design. Since it is known that most universal features are easier and safer for everyone to use, designers begin with the mandated minimums of existing laws and standards, and then go beyond them to achieve universal design.

Who Benefits from Universal Design?

Universal design ultimately benefits everyone. People who do not have an immediate need may not value universal design, even though later in life they will find universal design beneficial. This includes everyday products that become easier to use, such as kitchen utensils, door and cabinet hardware, as well as larger more visible print. For most consumers, universal design is unnoticeable, except that it is more convenient. Most people are surprised that universal design provides safer, more comfortable and more usable products and environments for all, while allowing some users the ability to confidently remain in place at times of temporary disability and as abilities diminish with age.

adjustable height lavatory counter-top and cabinets

Recent studies confirm these ideas. According to the National Council on Seniors Housing (NCSH), the active adults market (55 to 64) is one of the hottest markets in the nation. This market segment is affluent, healthier and independent; they tend to look for universal design features in homes where they can "age in place." Lifestyle sales, such as universally designed homes, promote blending with the community, yet enhancing real value with the types of features most often needed by seniors.

Universal Design in Housing

The idea for universal design in housing was recognized when accessible features were found to benefit others in the home. For example, raising electrical receptacles to 15 inches or 18 inches above the floor eliminates the need to bend over as far, making it more comfortable for everyone, or more universal. Some universal features make common activities easier for all: Moving day is facilitated in houses with stepless entrances and wider doors and hallways. Some universal design features create new and unique experiences. For example, well-designed bathrooms with extra floor space are perceived as luxurious and can accommodate furniture or other storage. A chair, bookcase, towel rack or storage shelf can give bathrooms a noticeable elegance. But these items can easily be removed if the space is needed to accommodate a family member or friend.

Universal design in housing far exceeds the minimum specifications of legislated barrier-free and accessible mandates. Universal design in housing applies universal design principles to all spaces, features and aspects of houses and creates homes that are usable by people of all ages and abilities. Some features of universally designed homes are adjustable to meet particular needs or needs that change as family members age, yet allow the home to remain marketable. Universal design has the unique quality that, when done well, it is invisible.

Examples of Universal Features

Many features and attributes help make a home universal. One that must be included is a level entrance. A feature called the "earth berm and bridge" is one way to make up the difference in elevation between the house and street. A gentle sloping walkway is designed using an attractive retaining wall and landscaping. Soil is pushed up to the front of the house at the foundation and a bridge spans the gap to the gently sloping sidewalk. Other features at the main entrance can include handrails, a package shelf, overhead covering and side windows to provide visual contact with guests as they arrive.

Exterior doors should all be 36 inches wide. Inside the home, interior passages and closet doors should provide at least a 32-inch clear opening. This allows easy maneuvering for people who use mobility aids, for moving furniture or for two people passing in the hall. Lever-style hardware used throughout the house makes opening doors easy for people with limited hand function or whose hands are full. Home controls, such as the thermostat, should have large visible displays and should be mounted at convenient heights for children and adults.

Using the same floor level throughout the first floor is a design element that everyone can appreciate. If there is a second floor, stairs should be wide enough to allow later installation of a stair lift. Handrails that extend at the top and bottom of the stairs provide added support. Contrasting treads and risers benefit people with low vision and everyone when the lighting is dim. In some cases, homeowners may want to consider space to add an elevator later on.

Well-executed universal design integrates many less obvious strategies, as well. For example, thoughtful attention to window placement can reduce glare, and careful selection of materials can improve air quality and address chemical-sensitivity issues.

upstairs closet

removable floor

stacked closets, storage, or pantry spaces with easy to remove floor system for use as shaft for residential elevator, if needed

downstairs closet

Many features can make the kitchen more universal and thus easier to use for everyone. Multiple work surfaces at different heights accommodate standing and seated users, as well as tall and short people. Contrasting counter edges define the edge of the counter and can be used to surround the sink basin. Open loop handles on all cabinet hardware minimizes fine finger manipulation. Seated users will find open knee space under the sink and cooktop helpful. A raised dishwasher minimizes bending to load and unload. Full extension drawers provide deep storage with easy access for all users. Faucets with lever handles and mounted at the side of the basin help minimize reach distance. Side-by-side refrigerators provide easy access to the freezer and refrigerator areas.

The bathroom is another area that benefits from universal design. Dual lavatories, one low with open knee space and a second at conventional height with a base cabinet below, provide flexible use for the homeowner. Grab bars can be included during construction, or added later if reinforcement (wall blocking) is provided. Clear floor space–a 5-foot turning radius–provides adequate room for someone who uses a wheelchair to safely transfer to the toilet. Bathing can be done in a conventional tub with an integral fold-down seat or a walk-in shower stall, both with an adjustable height showerhead. Controls set to the outside of the tub or shower allow easier and safer bathing.

Conclusion

For universal design to become common practice rather than the exception, it must become more widely accepted as a beneficial concept for everyone. Universal design needs to be adopted by the housing industry as part of common practice in developing consumer products and new construction. Although it is growing in understanding and acceptance, the industries that produce the built environment are large and complex. Changes within the system will take time.

The impact of recent civil rights legislation and a growing aging population has increased consciousness among designers, building owners and manufacturers about the rights of people with a range of abilities and the requirements for more accessible public and private places. People are disabled by situations and attitudes; a designer can meet the letter of the law, follow the details of the standards and still not create an enabling environment.

As we move into the new millennium, demand for better design will only increase. The plans and housing products featured in this book represent the state-of-the-art in universal design. We hope you find solutions here that facilitate a fulfilling lifestyle, not just today but for many years to come.

A Home For All Reasons

A home that incorporates the concepts of true universal design should be indistinguishable from any other home. It should not look contrived or dated, nor should it sacrifice balance, beauty and comfort for accessibility. The Christopher Grobbell residence, designed by Frank Salamone of Newline Design, is a premier example of the ultimate in universality.

Enclosing over 4,000 square feet of living space, this gracious, spacious home contains the very essence of good design and allows mobility, easy livability and plenty of space to work and entertain. Doorways and hallways are wide, living spaces are open and all areas of the home are easily reached, maneuverable and light-filled.

The wide central foyer is reached from a stepless columned porch with double doors and leads to the massive great room where wall-to-ceiling windows paint

Christopher Grobbel, at home, surrounded in elegant universal design.

A study in gorgeous contemporary universal design, the Christopher Grobbel home is masterfully planned and pleasing to the eye.

Photos: Bob Greenspan

A double-door entry opens to a two-story foyer with dramatic lighting and tiled floor.

The skylit great room is open to the foyer and features a half-round aquarium, a warm hearth, floor-to-ceiling windows, a continuation of the foyer's tiled floor and maneuverable spaces.

the space with light. Both the foyer and the great room are naturally lit by generous skylights contained in the second-story ceiling. A circular aquarium in the great room echoes the kitchen/nook area, which is also circular and holds a center island. Wide aisles, under-counter drawers, seated work spaces and adjustable work areas make the kitchen a gourmet's heaven. The center island features dual-height seating and bright lighting above.

A study on the right side of the plan is reached via a short staircase, or the installed elevator, and features double doors and built-in bookshelves for convenience. Beyond the columned hallway is a powder room, a walk-in closet and the formal dining room, which is open to the great room through a wide entry. A laundry room with service porch, built-in ironing center and cabinets finds efficiency near the entry to the three-car garage.

The master suite and one family bedroom occupy the left side of the plan. Bedroom 2 features a walk-in closet, built-in bookshelves and a private bath. The master suite is designed for complete luxury, with a tray ceiling, His and Hers dressing areas and closets, and, in the bath, a

Work areas in the kitchen are arranged in a circular pattern for convenience and enclose an island counter with dual heights. The sink, range and some counter spaces are at seated height for easy use.

Just to the right of the entry, the elevator serves as an accessible option to stairs leading to the study and to second-floor bedrooms.

Handy for guests, the powder room opens off the hallway to the dining room and is complemented by a lighted art niche.

The master bath is posh with modern amenities: a raised whirlpool tub, separate His and Hers areas, and a curbless shower with seat, handheld showerhead and wall of glass block.

Wonderfully open areas define the master bedroom, which is cheered by a fireplace that ties to the one in the great room.

curbless shower with seat and a separate whirlpool tub. The walk in closets in the master suite include fully adjustable closet systems. Clerestory windows infuse the suite with soft, ambient light.

The second floor, reached via the elevator or a short set of stairs, holds two additional bedrooms and a full bath. ◙

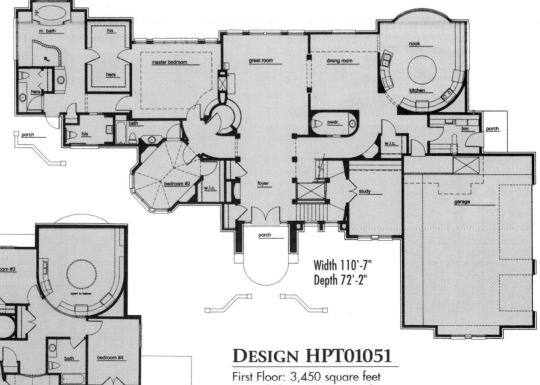

Width 110'-7"
Depth 72'-2"

DESIGN HPT01051

First Floor: 3,450 square feet
Second Floor: 750 square feet
Total: 4,200 square feet

Price Tier: C1

Remodeling for Universal Design

by Louis Tenenbaum

Design HPT01034 on page 93.

Access to products and universal design ideas such as those offered in *Products and Plans for Universal Homes* is essential. But creating a teamwork atmosphere is also a critical component in a successful remodeling project—perhaps even more so when the project involves universal design. The team is made up of the client and his family, along with the design and construction personnel that are hired for the project. The design and construction personnel must be people you trust and with whom you will be comfortable working over a long period of time in sometimes difficult situations.

How do you find the right people for your team? Start with referrals from friends, neighbors and agencies. Look for designers and contractors who are interested in universal design. They are likely to bring the most enthusiasm to your project. You must have confidence in their abilities and experience before you hire them—so don't hesitate to ask about their experience. If it is not clear how experi-

enced they are from referral sources ask for a list of previous clients you might interview. When talking to previous clients encourage them to speak openly about their opinions of the designer or contractor while answering your questions.

Designers and contractors should be interested in problem solving. They should demonstrate through their portfolio and references that they have the skills to work with standard materials, but also have the imagination to use their experience and talents to think and to work outside the box of standard practice. This is most important in universal design and accessibility. Universal design is not rocket science, nevertheless it often requires an imaginative use of space and materials to achieve its unique design goals within your budget.

Once deciding on your design and construction team, you can further enhance the project flow by following some simple guidelines. To get good results, you need to provide good information. The other team members need to listen carefully hoping to identify any special needs or wants. For example, curbless showers are common in accessible homes. However if you need a therapeutic bath or just love to soak in the tub, then having just a curbless shower with no tub is not the right solution. Remember that designers' and contractors' ideas and experience are their most valuable assets. Use them to work with you on the design and product identification because this is when you need their experience most.

Team Members for a Universal Remodeling Project

Client—can be an individual or couple but may also include:
    other family members such as adult children
    medical people such as doctors, nurses
        Occupational or Physical therapists
    social professionals such as a social worker or
        geriatric care manager
    family advocate such as an eldercare attorney or
        trust officer

Designer—often an architect or other trained
        draftsperson
    interior designer
    contractor/designer

A good early client task is to write a list of goals (called a "program") for the project. Jot notes over a few weeks, then collate, edit and prioritize the list. Some items will be "must haves," some "nice to have" and some will be out-and-out dreams. List them all. Even items that you do not think you can afford or fit may influence the design. You must also list things you don't like. This is particularly important in remodeling. Existing elements that you may not like will be balanced against their useful value.

Make your budget known to the team, but resist the temptation to focus on cost. Have patience as you work with your team to brainstorm solutions in order to create some sketches or plan views for the project (these initial plan views are called "schematics"). Don't short-circuit the team's creativity by predicting the result. The initial and obvious solutions may be the best ones, but you can only tell this by comparison with some other solutions.

Once the general design and scope of the work is decided, permit drawings and specifications can be developed. This is when the details of the structural and mechanical work are figured out, and when the materials are chosen. This phase of the preparation is called "design development." Check back to your program notes at this time to make sure that compromises you have made are things that you can live without. The project will not be a success if one of your "must haves" is not included. Design development is also the stage when pricing can be defined with more confidence. And, remember, you can influence cost by making good decisions. For instance, if you pick vinyl flooring for the kitchen, it will likely cost less than ceramic tile. However, don't be too stubborn about specified items. You must make the decisions that allow the construction work to begin. If you decide you must have the highest quality products, then you may have to reduce the scope of the work.

Once the final plans are drawn and all details regarding products worked out, a contract can be arrived at for the work. At this stage you should be able to confirm that what you are expecting to have as a finished product is the same as what has been designed and is to be built. If this cannot be confirmed do not begin construction. Disputes and disappointments most often occur when the client looks at the finished product and says "I didn't think it was going to look like THAT!"

Once construction begins, remember that change orders or "extras" have a serious impact on a project and its timeliness. Changes must be considered carefully to make sure their effect does not impact other significant elements and goals. They must be priced accurately and profitably or they will throw a budget into a tailspin. They also disturb the construction process, causing delays and missed deadlines that affect all aspects of the job. An old adage in the construction business is "measure twice, cut once." You might relate this to your project to insure that your remodeling project is successfully completed—prepare and design with patience, then build. If your planning is effective, the construction process will make your dreams come true.⊠

Next Generation Universal Home

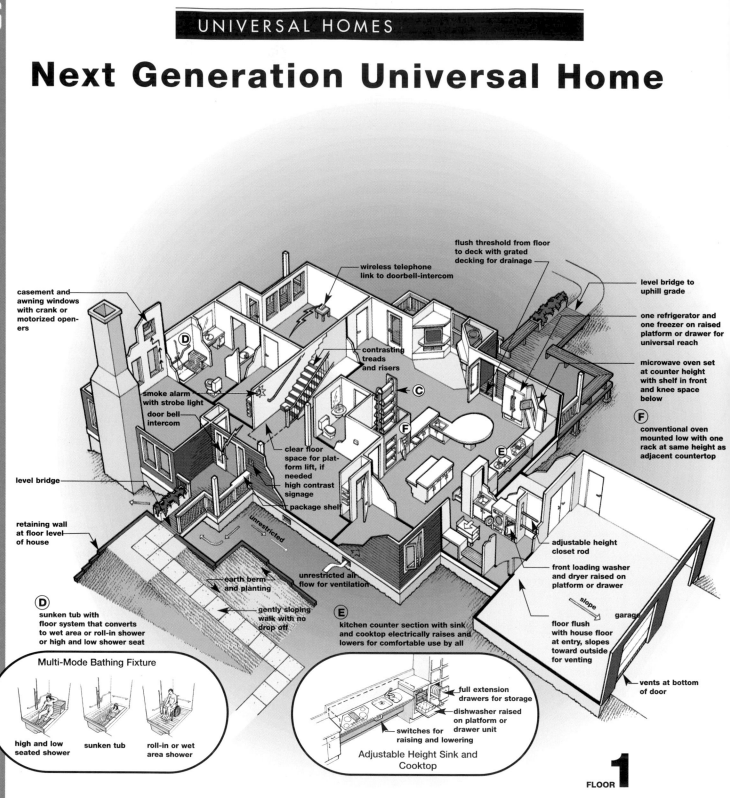

casement and awning windows with crank or motorized openers

smoke alarm with strobe light

door bell intercom

level bridge

retaining wall at floor level of house

wireless telephone link to doorbell-intercom

contrasting treads and risers

clear floor space for platform lift, if needed

high contrast signage

package shelf

unrestricted

earth berm and planting

unrestricted air flow for ventilation

gently sloping walk with no drop off

flush threshold from floor to deck with grated decking for drainage

level bridge to uphill grade

one refrigerator and one freezer on raised platform or drawer for universal reach

microwave oven set at counter height with shelf in front and knee space below

(F) conventional oven mounted low with one rack at same height as adjacent countertop

adjustable height closet rod

front loading washer and dryer raised on platform or drawer

slope

floor flush with house floor at entry, slopes toward outside for venting

garage

vents at bottom of door

(D) sunken tub with floor system that converts to wet area or roll-in shower or high and low shower seat

(E) kitchen counter section with sink and cooktop electrically raises and lowers for comfortable use by all

Multi-Mode Bathing Fixture

high and low seated shower

sunken tub

roll-in or wet area shower

Adjustable Height Sink and Cooktop

full extension drawers for storage

dishwasher raised on platform or drawer unit

switches for raising and lowering

FLOOR 1

Major funding provided by the National Institute on Disability and Rehabilitation Research, US Department of Education

www.design.ncsu.edu/cud

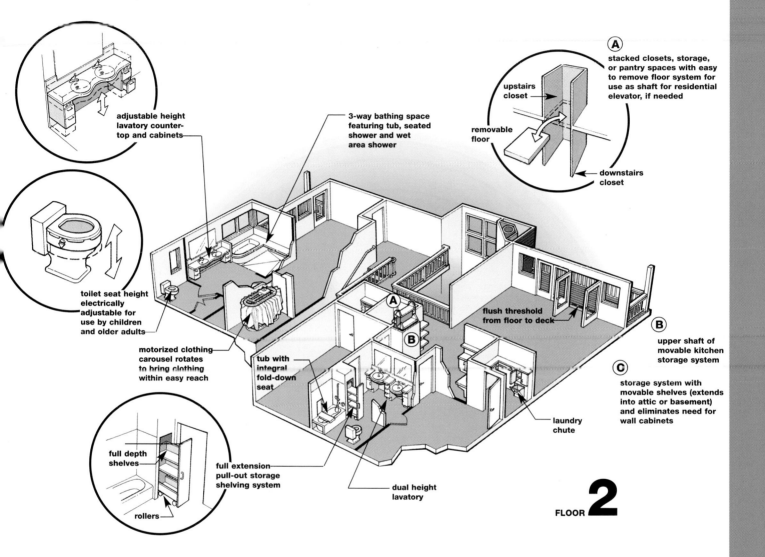

adjustable height lavatory counter-top and cabinets

toilet seat height electrically adjustable for use by children and older adults

3-way bathing space featuring tub, seated shower and wet area shower

A stacked closets, storage, or pantry spaces with easy to remove floor system for use as shaft for residential elevator, if needed

upstairs closet

removable floor

downstairs closet

motorized clothing carousel rotates to bring clothing within easy reach

tub with integral fold-down seat

flush threshold from floor to deck

B upper shaft of movable kitchen storage system

C storage system with movable shelves (extends into attic or basement) and eliminates need for wall cabinets

full depth shelves

full extension pull-out storage shelving system

dual height lavatory

laundry chute

rollers

FLOOR **2**

The Next Generation Universal Home is a model developed by the Center for Universal Design at North Carolina State University. It shows an incorporation of the best features that might be included in a universal home and takes into account various lifestyle changes, age differences, height differences and ability differences that could occur in an average household. Many of the items outlined in this three-dimensional model are available from companies listed in the Products grids on pages 25-58. Other items are ones that can be devised at the building stage and can be discussed with your general contractor before beginning your home building project: sloping walks, retaining wall at floor level of house and level bridges. Use this model as an idea generator for the kinds of convenient products you'd like to include in your universal home.

Universal Product Characteristics

Below is a list of universal features to consider when selecting home architectural products, appliances and fixtures. Few products will have all of the listed features. Products usually have a combination of particular features, some of which may be especially useful to you. Use this as a starting point in your search for products that will work for you.

Note that installation location can make a difference in a product's usability. For example, a side-hinged oven can be useful for many people, avoiding the need to reach over a hot oven door to retrieve items. Mounted too low or too high, the door swing advantage is compromised by a difficult reach placement.

Product	Controls	Display/Labels	Other Features
Microwaves	■ Raised, cupped or otherwise detectable by touch ■ Clear relationship to function (how it works and what it operates) ■ Can be used with low effort and with minimum finger use ■ Minimal programming required	■ High-contrast graphics (white on black) ■ Large-size lettering (¼" high) ■ Redundant signals, visual and audible alarms	■ Microwave/convection combination ■ No lip at front edge
Ranges	■ Front- or side-mounted ■ Raised, cupped or otherwise detectable by touch ■ Clear relationship to function (how it works and what it operates) ■ Can be used with low effort and with minimum finger use	■ High-contrast graphics (white on black) ■ Large-size lettering (¼" high) ■ Redundant signals, visual and audible alarms	■ Offset burners ■ Smooth cooktop ■ "Cool" cooktop burners
Stove Tops	■ Front- or side-mounted ■ Raised, cupped or otherwise detectable by touch ■ Clear relationship to function (how it works and what it operates) ■ Can be used with low effort and with minimum finger use	■ High-contrast graphics (white on black) ■ Large-size lettering (¼" high) ■ Redundant signals, visual and audible alarms ■ Color contrast with counter	■ Offset burners ■ Smooth cooktop ■ "Cool" cooktop burners
Wall Ovens	■ Clear relationship to function (how it works and what it operates) ■ Can be used with low effort and with minimum finger use	■ High-contrast graphics (white on black) ■ Large-size lettering (¼" high) ■ Redundant signals, visual and audible alarms	■ Side-hinged door
Refrigerators	■ Handles that can be used with low effort and with minimum finger use ■ Full-height handles ■ Reachable interior controls	■ High-contrast graphics (white on black) ■ Large-size lettering (¼" high)	■ Side-by-side or freezer-under style ■ Pull-out shelves ■ Adjustable interior shelves ■ Water- and ice-in-the-door feature ■ At least 180° opening doors ■ Under counter in drawer ■ Beverage/snack dispenser

Product	Controls	Display/Labels	Other Features
Dishwasher	■ Raised, cupped or otherwise detectable by touch ■ Clear relationship to function (how it works and what it operates) ■ Can be used with low effort and with minimum finger use ■ Minimal programming required	■ High-contrast graphics (white on black) ■ Large-size lettering (¼" high) ■ Redundant signals, visual and audible alarms	■ Under counter in drawer ■ Adjustable racks
Clothes Washer	■ Front-mounted controls ■ Raised, cupped or otherwise detectable by touch ■ Clear relationship to function (how it works and what it operates) ■ Can be used with low effort and with minimum finger use	■ High-contrast graphics (white on black) ■ Large-size lettering (¼" high) ■ Redundant signals, visual and audible alarms	■ Easy-to-understand instructions ■ Smaller sizes can be easier to reach into ■ Front-loading ■ Side-hinged ■ Front detergent loading
Clothes Dryer	■ Front-mounted controls ■ Raised, cupped or otherwise detectable by touch ■ Clear relationship to function (how it works and what it operates) ■ Can be used with low effort and with minimum finger use	■ High-contrast graphics (white on black) ■ Large-size lettering (¼" high) ■ Redundant signals, visual and audible alarms	■ Easy-to-understand instructions ■ Smaller sizes can be easier to reach into ■ Side-hinged ■ Front lint screen
Kitchen Cabinets	■ Loop or touch-latch hardware	■ Intermittent glass doors	■ Pull-out shelving ■ Pull-out cutting boards ■ Lazy Susans in corners ■ High toe-space option (9" x 6") ■ Cabinet height options from 27½" to 40½" ■ Lighted cabinet interior option ■ Formaldehyde-free construction ■ Pull-out pantries ■ Open storage racks
Kitchen Sinks		■ Color contrast with counter	■ Shallow (from under 6½" to 7½") ■ Rear-mounted drain ■ Disposal or two-basin sink
Bathroom Sinks		■ Color contrast with counter	■ Shallow (from under 6½" to 7½") ■ Rear-mounted drain
Faucets	■ Single levers, crosses or loops ■ Non-slip textures ■ Easy to control flow rate ■ Easy to adjust temperature ■ Peddle-operated option ■ Infra-red motion sensing ■ Side-mounted	■ Easy to distinguish hot from cold with letters and color ■ Color-contrasting handles	■ Built-in spray/removable spray
Grab Bars		■ Color contrast with wall	■ 1¼" to 1½" diameter only ■ Finishing choices including colors

Product	Controls	Display/Labels	Other Features
Toilets	■ Can be used with low effort and with minimum finger use ■ Flush control on open side ■ Infra-red motion sensing		■ 17" to 19" seat-height option ■ Elongated bowl
Shower/Tub Mix Valves	■ Adjustable temperature levels ■ Easy-to-grip handle ■ Hand-held shower with push-button on hand unit/69" minimum hose	■ Easy to distinguish hot from cold with letters and color ■ Temperature display	■ Anti-scald features
Home Automation Controls	■ Remote control ■ Large-button, hand-held unit ■ Easy to set relationship between transmitter and receiver	■ High-contrast graphics (white on black) ■ Large-size lettering (¼" high) ■ Redundant signals, visual and audible alarms	■ Remote sensing ■ Computer or TV access
Closet			■ Lighted closet interior ■ Adjustable height closet rod or rods mounted at two heights OR ■ Adjustable closet system ■ Recessed floor track (if used) ■ Walk-in capability
Door Handles	■ Lever type ■ 5" long		■ Smooth edges ■ Lever returns close to door (turnback)
Windows	■ Can be opened with one hand, closed fist	■ Hardware color-contrasting with casement	■ Can be outfitted with power opener ■ Casement/awning type ■ Locks and cranks no higher than 44"
Door Locksets	■ Large deadbolt handle ■ Easy to turn ■ Mortise style (integral latch and lock)	■ Easy-to-see/night lit ■ "Locked" indicator	■ Remote electrical operation
Light Switches	■ Rocker panel or touch controls allow low-effort use	■ Color contrast with wall	■ Glow-in-the-dark for night use ■ Motion detecting features increase safety
Lifts/Elevators	■ Controls on both sides of cab ■ Controls no higher than 44" ■ Raised, cupped or otherwise detectable by touch ■ Can be used with low effort and with minimum finger use		■ At least 32" x 48" interior floor space ■ Automatic opening doors

HOUSMART
innovations ℠

Smart design. Better living.

Order the
Home Design Catalog
That's as *Unique*
as You Are!

HOUSMART *innovations*℠ uses a sophisticated computer program to match your preferences with innovative home building products, home safety tips, and design ideas evaluated by internationally recognized universal design experts.

Follow the instructions to receive your customized catalog of home design, building, and remodeling products and ideas selected just for you.

Instructions

To order your custom catalog, simply:

1 Fill out the Getting to Know You section.

2 Tell us your lifestyle objectives.

3 Tell us your personal considerations.

4 Send this form and your payment to us.

1 Getting To Know You

Name _____

Address _____ Apt# _____

City _____ State _____ ZIP _____

Phone Number (_____) _____

Are You (check one): ❑ building a new home ❑ remodeling ❑ investigating

2 Lifestyle
Select up to 7 *lifestyle objectives* you expect. Select by checking the corresponding box. ☑

❑ **Convenience**
Simplifies tasks and chores

❑ **Hospitality**
Enhances guest interaction and comfort

❑ **Style**
Reflects design excellence and aesthetics

❑ **Ease of Use**
Easy to operate and understand

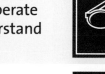
❑ **Image**
Reflects quality and personal achievement

❑ **Technology**
Provides technological innovations

❑ **Easy-care**
Low maintenance finishes

❑ **Low Cost/ No Cost**
Inexpensive or free ideas and solutions

❑ **Value**
Reflects strong cost/benefit relationship

❑ **Flexibility**
Adapts easily to different uses

❑ **Peace of Mind**
Enhances security and monitoring capabilities

Please Turn to
Next Page
➡

3 Personal

Select up to 10 *personal considerations* your home might adjust for. Select by checking the corresponding box. ☑

 ☐ **Balance**
Enhancing stability while standing and moving

 ☐ **Lighting**
Enhancing vision in low light and light changes

 ☐ **Speech**
Enhancing speech and making it comprehensible

 ☐ **Chair Use**
Managing sitting and rising from chair

 ☐ **Memory**
Enhancing memory for processing

 ☐ **Stair Use**
Easing movement on stairs

 ☐ **Chemical Sensitivity**
Accommodating sensitivities

 ☐ **Mobility**
Managing movement over objects

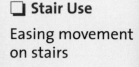 ☐ **Stamina**
Easing light and moderate on-going activity

 ☐ **Depth Perception**
Discriminating surface changes

 ☐ **Reaching**
Enhancing reaching above or beyond body

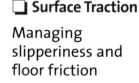 ☐ **Steadiness**
Moving objects without spills or dropping

 ☐ **Glare**
Enhancing vision to accommodate glaring lights

 ☐ **Rising**
Managing rising from floor, tub or bed

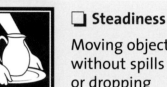 ☐ **Surface Traction**
Managing slipperiness and floor friction

 ☐ **Hand Dexterity**
Hand use, strength and movement

 ☐ **Seeing At A Distance**
Seeing objects far away

☐ **Temperature Awareness**
Detecting cold and hot

 ☐ **Hearing**
Enhancing sound and understanding its meaning

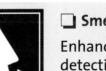 ☐ **Seeing Up Close**
Seeing close objects and reading

☐ **Wheelchair Use**
Seated movement

☐ **Lifting/ Carrying**
Easing movement of objects

☐ **Smell**
Enhancing odor detection

Questions?
Toll Free
1.877.604.0937

---

4 Attach your $49.00 payment and send with this form to us:

Your customized catalog costs only $45.00 plus $4.00 shipping and handling. Make your check or money order payable to: **PSC - HOUSMART**, enclose the completed form, and send to:

The Philip Stephen Companies (PSC)
2845 Hamline Avenue North, Suite 222
Roseville, MN 55113

Please allow three weeks for processing.

How to Use *Products & Plans* for *Universal Homes*

Building a home requires thousands of products, some standard, some not-so-standard. When building a universal home, the range of products becomes even more extensive and perhaps elusive. Searching for these products, or, in fact, even discovering whether or not they exist, can be time-consuming and frustrating. This guide, *Products and Plans for Universal Homes,* was developed to assist in finding those unique products that pertain to universal design. Though a huge portion of the materials used in universal homes is standard and common to all homes, many of the products are specific to universal homes. It is these products that this book catalogs.

The first of its kind, *Products and Plans for Universal Homes* defines those products that are found in the very best universal homes. Encompassing over 450 manufacturers and suppliers and over 1,700 products, it is the most complete, detailed guide for finding products for the universal home.

The guide is easy to use. Products are organized into sixteen main color-coded product categories and further defined by more specific products within those categories. Looking for a source for pedal faucets for the bath? Turn to Plumbing, Faucets and Fixtures and find the product heading foot-pedal bath faucets for a list of sources. The listing, in many cases, will indicate how the products are sold— either direct to you or through local dealers and distributors.

To contact that source for ordering or to find a retailer in your area, turn to the Manufacturers and Suppliers Index starting on page 116 for complete address and telephone information about each of the suppliers. In some cases, there is also a FAX number and an E-mail or Internet address.

We've also included a useful Product Index on page 127, with cross references to give you the most complete sourcebook for universal home products.

Products: Read across to see what products a company offers.

Manufacturers and Suppliers Index: Here you'll find addresses, phone numbers (many toll free), FAX number and more for over 450 companies. See page 116.

Product Index: Refer to this index if you're looking for a specific product and don't know where to find it. See page 127.

Looking for additional reference material? Check the Services and Resources Appendix on page 115, which lists companies such as architectural services and trade associations. The Active Living Devices Appendix contains companies that offer products for assisted living, not necessarily architectural products.

But the book doesn't just contain product information. There is also a very special section of over 50 home plans that feature universal design starting on page 59. Each of these plans has been designed specifically to meet the criteria of a well-executed universal home. They contain many of the following special features:

- Flush entries
- 5' turning radius in the baths
- Wider stairs for chair lift
- Roll-under sinks in kitchens and baths
- Wider doorways
- Wider hallways
- Hardboard backer in baths for grab bars
- Off-set plumbing on fixtures
- And much more!

And even better, complete construction blueprints are available for every home. Turn to pages 110-113 for complete order information.

Design HPT01015, page 74

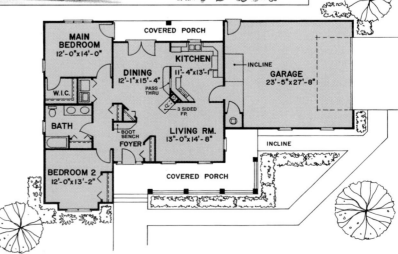

Appliances

COMPANY	accessible compact kitchens	automated/timer control range hoods	batch-feed disposers (operational only with lid in place)	clothes dryers front-loading with front-mounted controls	clothes washers front-loading with front-mounted controls	cooktops with "cool touch" burners	cooktops with offset burners and front-mounted controls	cooktops with smooth surface and front-mounted controls	dishwashers in drawer under counter	dishwashers with one-touch operation	microwave/convection oven combinations	outdoor grills with front-mounted controls	ranges with "cool touch" burners	ranges with front-mounted controls and smooth surfaces	ranges with offset burners and front-mounted controls	refrigerator/freezers in under-counter drawer	refrigerators—mini	refrigerators side-by-side with in-door water/ice dispensers	refrigerators with slide-out lower-drawer freezers	"talking" appliances	wall ovens with side-swing door	Local dealer/distributor	Factory-direct
Access-Ability	■			■	■	■	■	■	■	■		■	■	■	■	■	■		■	■			■
Accessible Designs/Adjustable Systems	■																					■	■
Amana Appliances				■				■			■			■				■	■			■	
Anaheim Mfg. Co.			■																			■	
Appliances Intl.				■	■					■													■
Cardinal Homes, Inc.							■	■						■				■	■			■	
CMi Worldwide	■																			■		■	■
Dwyer Products Corp.	■																					■	■
DYNASTY Range												■										■	
Empire Comfort Systems												■										■	
Franke Consumer Products/Kitchen Sys. Div.			■																			■	
GE Appliances			■	■	■	■	■	■		■	■		■	■		■	■	■				■	
Hunter Technology												■										■	
Independent Living Aids, Inc.											■									■			■
Jenn-Air						■				■	■			■					■			■	
Kanalflakt		■																				■	
Marvel Industries																	■					■	
Miele Inc.	■			■	■				■													■	
M-T Systems LLC				■																		■	■
Renato Specialty Products												■										■	■
Richlund Enterprises				■	■											■	■	■				■	■
Sharp Electronics Corp.										■												■	
Sub-Zero Freezer Co.																■	■	■	■			■	
Viking Range Corp.			■						■				■		■			■	■			■	

See listing for Manufactures and Suppliers Index for address and phone information.

Cabinetry

COMPANY	PRODUCTS													SALES	
	180-degree door-swing hinges	automated shelf-counter movement systems	expanded toe-kick space (min. 8" h x 4" d)	formaldehyde-free construction	lower-mount wall oven cabinets (about 30" mount)	pull-out shelf trays	pull-out table-top work areas	raised dishwasher cabinets (12" h min. mount)	reconfigurable component systems	short base cabinets (max. 32½")	sink or cooktop mounting platforms open underneath	tall base cabinets (min. 38")	transparent shelving for increased light	Local dealer/distributor	Factory-direct
Access-Ability	■	■	■	■	■	■	■	■	■	■	■	■	■		■
Accessible Designs/Adjustable Systems		■								■				■	■
Accessiblity By Design	■		■		■	■	■			■	■	■	■		■
ALNO Network USA/Boston Design Center	■	■	■	■	■	■	■	■	■	■	■	■	■	■	
Amerock Corp.					■				■					■	■
Architectural Products by Outwater	■														■
Aristokraft			■		■					■				■	
Auton Motorized Systems		■													
Birchcraft Kitchens	■		■		■	■	■			■	■	■		■	
Cabinet Studio	■			■	■					■	■			■	■
Canac Kitchens	■		■		■	■		■		■				■	
Canyon Creek Cabinet Co.			■		■	■	■			■	■	■			
Cardinal Homes, Inc.								■		■				■	
Central Lock and Hardware Supply Co.	■					■	■							■	■
Curvoflite Stairs and Millwork	■		■		■	■	■			■		■		■	■
Custom Wood Products	■		■	■	■	■	■			■	■	■		■	
Decorá		■		■	■		■			■		■		■	
Decora Systems					■									■	■
Dura Supreme	■		■		■		■			■	■	■		■	
Feeny Mfg. Co.					■				■					■	■
Fieldstone Cabinetry	■		■		■	■	■	■	■					■	
Gibco Services										■		■		■	
Grass America	■				■									■	
Hafele America					■	■								■	
HDI					■	■								■	
Holiday Kitchens/(A Div. of Mastercraft Ind.)	■		■	■	■	■	■	■		■	■	■		■	
Home Crest Corp.	■		■		■	■		■		■					
IXL Cabinets/(A Div. of Triangle Pacific)			■	■	■	■				■	■	■		■	■
Kohler Co.									■					■	■
Kolson	■													■	■
KraftMaid Cabinetry 1	■		■		■	■	■	■		■	■	■	■	■	
LesCare Kitchens	■		■		■	■	■	■		■	■	■		■	
Marsh Furniture Co.	■				■					■				■	
Mid Continent Cabinetry/Div. of Norcraft Cos.		■			■					■		■		■	
Monterey Shelf									■					■	■
Neil Kelly Signature Cabinets	■		■		■	■	■	■		■	■	■		■	■

See listing for Manufactures and Suppliers Index for address and phone information.

Dura Supreme . . .
The Answer to the Universal Question.

Whether you need to accommodate young children, aging parents, or a physical disability, Dura Supreme cabinetry fits your lifestyle. We recommend working with a designer that can create a kitchen or bath with your personal needs in mind.

This custom kitchen is shown in Rigel Panel door style with Champagne Sand finish on maple.

Universal features include
- Pocket doors at clean-up and food preparation areas
- Raised dishwasher and lowered ovens for user-friendly access
- User friendly cabinetry handles and appliance controls
- Recessed, open area below the microwave

DURA SUPREME
"Excellence in Handcrafted Cabinetry"

300 Dura Drive, P.O. Box K
Howard Lake, MN 55349
Phone: 320-543-3872
Fax 320-543-3310

Cabinetry

COMPANY	180-degree door-swing hinges	automated shelf-counter movement systems	expanded toe-kick space (min. 8" h x 4" d)	formaldehyde-free construction	lower-mount wall oven cabinets (about 30" mount)	pull-out shelf trays	pull-out table-top work areas	raised dishwasher cabinets (12" h min. mount)	reconfigurable component systems	short base cabinets (max. 32½")	sink or cooktop mounting platforms open underneath	tall base cabinets (min. 38")	transparent shelving for increased light	Local dealer/distributor	Factory-direct
Plain & Fancy Custom Cabinetry	■		■		■	■	■	■	■	■	■	■		■	
Rynone Mfg. Corp.	■	■	■					■	■	■	■			■	
Selby Furniture Hardware Co.		■												■	
SierraPine Ltd.				■										■	■
Vance Industries						■								■	
Wellborn Cabinet	■		■			■	■	■		■	■	■		■	
Wood Technology	■													■	
Wood-Mode	■		■		■	■	■	■	■	■	■	■		■	

See listing for Manufactures and Suppliers Index for address and phone information.

[1] Awards: Passport Series Cabinetry
Certified for Universal Design by the Institute for Technology Development
Named "Best New Product for Mature Markets" by the American Society on Aging
Won 1998 "Product Innovator Awards" from *Kitchen and Bath Business*
Named one of "Best New Products, 1998" by *Today's Homeowner* magazine

Countertops

COMPANY	adjustable-height countertops	heat-resistant surfaces	high color- or tactile-contrast counter edging	slip-resistant counter surfaces	PRODUCTS															Local dealer/distributor	Factory-direct
Access-Ability	■	■	■	■																	■
Accessible Designs/Adjustable Systems	■																			■	■
Accessiblity By Design	■	■	■	■																	■
ALNO Network USA/Boston Design Center		■																		■	
American Marazzi Tile		■																		■	
American Marble Industries/Kophaco Corp.		■	■																		

See listing for Manufactures and Suppliers Index for address and phone information.

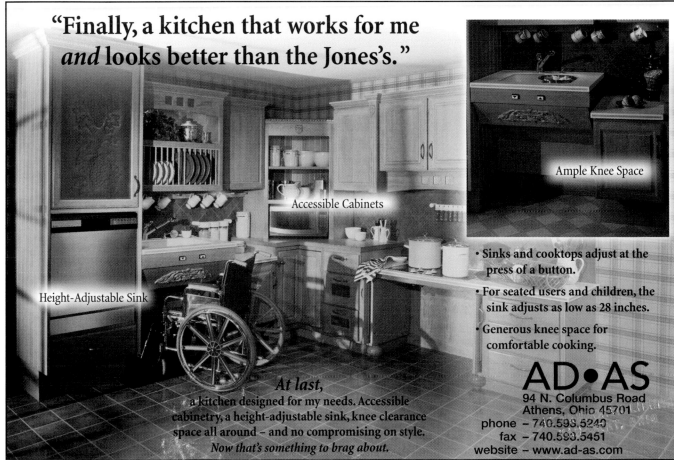

"Finally, a kitchen that works for me *and* looks better than the Jones's."

Height-Adjustable Sink

Accessible Cabinets

Ample Knee Space

- Sinks and cooktops adjust at the press of a button.
- For seated users and children, the sink adjusts as low as 28 inches.
- Generous knee space for comfortable cooking.

At last,
a kitchen designed for my needs. Accessible cabinetry, a height-adjustable sink, knee clearance space all around – and no compromising on style. *Now that's something to brag about.*

AD•AS
94 N. Columbus Road
Athens, Ohio 45701
phone – 740.593.5240
fax – 740.593.5451
website – www.ad-as.com

COMPANY	adjustable-height countertops	heat-resistant surfaces	high color- or tactile-contrast counter edging	slip-resistant counter surfaces	Local dealer/distributor	Factory-direct
Astracast		■	■	■	■	
Canital Granite		■			■	
Cardinal Homes, Inc.	■				■	
Central Lock and Hardware Supply Co.			■	■	■	
Coni Marble Mfg.	■		■	■	■	■
Crossville Ceramics Co.		■			■	
Dakota Granite		■			■	
Formica Corp.		■	■		■	
Hafele America	■				■	
Interceramic, USA		■			■	
Kepcor/SSI Tiles		■			■	■
Kuehn Bevel			■		■	
Latco Products		■			■	■
Lodestar/Statements in Stone		■	■		■	
LTS Ceramics		■			■	
Nevamar, Intl. Paper Co./Decorative Prod. Div.	■		■		■	
Rocktile Specialty Products				■	■	■
Rynone Mfg. Corp.	■	■	■	■	■	
The Structural Slate Co.		■			■	■
Summitville Tiles		■			■	
United States Ceramic Tile Co.		■			■	■
Universal Marble & Granite		■			■	
Vermont Marble Co.		■				
Walker & Zanger		■			■	
Westchester Marble & Granite		■			■	■
Wilsonart Intl.		■	■	■	■	

See listing for Manufactures and Suppliers Index for address and phone information.

Doors—Exterior

COMPANY	hinged sidelights	large-view door scopes	low-profile thresholds (½" max.)	motion-sensing openers	outswing doors with operable window in panel	power-operated openers	video-display door scopes	Local dealer/distributor	Factory-direct
ABC Seamless Siding	■							■	■
Access-Ability	■	■	■	■	■	■	■		■
Accessiblity By Design		■	■						■
Aiphone Communications						■			
ALNO Network USA/Boston Design Center	■	■	■					■	
Andersen Windows					■			■	
Benchmark Door Systems			■						
Bennett Industries	■							■	
Central Lock and Hardware Supply Co.		■	■	■		■	■	■	
Dorma Architectural Hardware					■			■	
Hartford Conservatories					■			■	■
The Hess Mfg. Co.					■			■	
Horton Automatics				■		■		■	
Huron Window Corp.	■				■			■	■
International Window/Maestro	■							■	
Jensen Medical		■				■			
Kaycan		■						■	
Kolbe & Kolbe Millwork Co.		■						■	
Lamson-Taylor Custom Doors	■	■	■						■
Logcrafters Log & Timber Homes	■	■			■	■			■
Norco Windows			■					■	
Northeast Window and Door Assn.	■	■	■	■	■	■	■		
Oakwood Classic & Custom Woodworks	■							■	■
Power Access Corp.						■		■	
Prime-Line Products Co.		■						■	
R & D Equipment 1			■					■	■
Sealeze			■					■	■
Semco Windows & Doors/Semling-Menke Co.			■					■	
Steelwood Doors	■							■	
Windsor Windows				■				■	
Yale Security Group			■	■		■	■	■	

See listing for Manufactures and Suppliers Index for address and phone information.

[1] Award: "Best in Iowa"— QVC Television (Sure Seal)

Doors—Interior

COMPANY	PRODUCTS					SALES	
	free swinging (or dual swinging)	integral decorative kick plates	pocket doors	power-operated openers	sound-insulated doors	Local dealer/distributor	Factory-direct
ABC Seamless Siding	■				■	■	■
Access-Ability	■	■					■
Accessiblity By Design	■	■			■		■
ALNO Network USA/Boston Design Center	■					■	
Bennett Industries	■					■	
Central Lock and Hardware Supply Co.		■				■	
Doorcraft	■				■	■	
Hafele America			■			■	
Hartford Conservatories	■					■	■
International Paper Co.	■						
Ledco	■					■	
Logcrafters Log & Timber Homes	■						■
Masonite Corp.	■					■	
Nevamar, Intl. Paper Co./Decorative Prod. Div.		■				■	
Northeast Window and Door Assn.	■	■			■	■	
Oakwood Classic & Custom Woodworks	■					■	■
Power Access Corp.				■		■	
Tri-Guards		■				■	
Woodfold-Marco Mfg.				■		■	

See listing for Manufactures and Suppliers Index for address and phone information.

Electrical & Lighting

COMPANY	door-activated light switches	flashing-light doorbells and alerting devices	fluorescent lighting	intercoms/communication devices	large, lighted toggle switches	natural lighting sources	photo-control/timer/remote-control switches	remote-control ceiling fans	stand-by generators	task lighting	whole-house control systems	Local dealer/distributor	Factory-direct
Access-Ability	■	■			■		■				■		■
Accessiblity By Design	■	■			■		■						■
Aiphone Communications		■		■									
ALKCO										■		■	
Alpha Communications		■		■								■	
Ameriphone		■		■								■	■
Ardee Lighting			■							■		■	
AVSI Automated Voice Systems				■								■	
Bird-X		■											
Braun Elevator Co.	■	■			■		■		■	■			■
Broan-NuTone					■		■					■	
Casablanca Fan Co.								■				■	
Central Lock and Hardware Supply Co.	■	■			■		■					■	
Centralite	■	■			■		■				■	■	
CMi Worldwide				■								■	■
d'ac Lighting			■							■		■	
Defiant Safe Co.											■	■	■
Eagle Electric Mfg. Co.				■								■	
Enertel Controls				■			■					■	■
Engelite Lighting 1										■		■	
First Alert Professional Security Systems											■	■	
Flos USA			■							■		■	
GE Company/GE Lighting			■							■		■	■
GINGER/GUSA										■		■	
Globe Fire Sprinkler Corp.											■	■	
GTE Corp.				■								■	■
Hafele America						■						■	
Halo Lighting/(A Brand of Cooper Lighting)										■		■	
Heatway											■	■	
Honeywell Home & Building Control		■		■			■				■	■	
Hubbell Lighting			■							■		■	
Independent Living Aids, Inc.		■											■
IntelliNet											■	■	
Kidde Fyrnetics		■		■								■	
Leviton Mfg.	■	■		■	■		■			■		■	
Lighting Services										■		■	

See listing for Manufactures and Suppliers Index for address and phone information.

Anyone Can

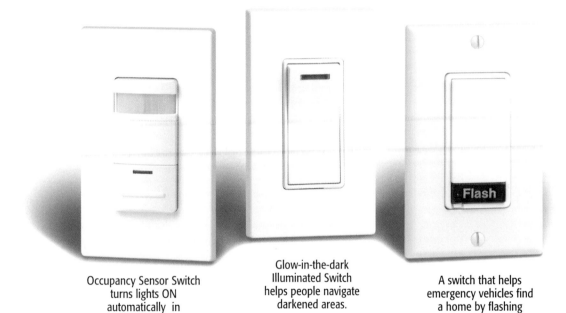

Use These Light Switches with Little or No Effort

Occupancy Sensor Switch
turns lights ON
automatically in
response to motion.

Glow-in-the-dark
Illuminated Switch
helps people navigate
darkened areas.

A switch that helps
emergency vehicles find
a home by flashing
exterior lights ON and OFF.

Leviton DECORA® products look great in any interior and make life easier for people of all ages and abilities. Decora switches are easier to use than traditional toggle style switches, requiring only a light tap on the rocker. Precision finger movement is not needed - the side or back of the hand, the elbow or shoulder can be used.

This series also includes timer switches, programmable controls, hand-held remote controls, table-top controls, dimmers, outlets, outdoor motion sensors and more. For a free Universal Design Products brochure or more information contact us at **800-323-8920** or visit us at **www.leviton.com**

Decora products have been recognized by the following organizations: The Center for Universal Design at North Carolina State University; The National Endowment for the Arts for "Excellence in Universal Design."

Building A Connected World

Electrical & Lighting

COMPANY	door-activated light switches	flashing-light doorbells and alerting devices	fluorescent lighting	intercoms/communication devices	large, lighted toggle switches	natural lighting sources	photo-control/timer/remote-control switches	remote-control ceiling fans	stand-by generators	task lighting	whole-house control systems	Local dealer/distributor	Factory-direct
Lightway Industries			■							■		■	
Luxo Corp.			■							■		■	
M & S Systems				■								■	
Miami-Carey Ltd.		■										■	
Napco Security Systems		■									■	■	
Nessen Lighting			■							■		■	
Newstamp Lighting Co.			■							■		■	■
OSRAM SYLVANIA			■							■		■	
Petmark Home Security Products		■										■	■
Point Electric										■		■	
Precision Multiple Controls							■					■	■
Prescolite-Moldcast			■							■		■	
Progress Lighting			■							■		■	
Raylux										■		■	
Robern										■		■	
Roberts Step-Lite Systems			■									■	
Smarthome.com							■				■		■
SmartLinc				■		■						■	
SOLATUBE Intl.						■						■	
Specialty Lighting			■							■		■	
Starfire Lighting			■							■		■	
Sure-Lites/(A Brand of Cooper Lighting)		■										■	
Sun Tunnel Skylights						■						■	
Swivelier										■		■	
Targetti USA			■							■		■	
Thomas Lighting/Consumer Div.			■							■		■	
Tivoli Industries			■							■		■	
Tork	■	■										■	
Tubular Skylighte, Inc.						■						■	■

See listing for Manufactures and Suppliers Index for address and phone information.

[1] 75% of all Canadian "Trillium" awards went to Engelite products for the last 4 years.

Flooring

COMPANY	cushioned flooring	floor leveling materials	glare-inhibiting matte finishes	low-cut pile (versus loop pile) carpeting (½" max. pile)	natural cork flooring	slip-resistant flooring surfaces	wear-resistant flooring	Local dealer/distributor	Factory-direct
Access-Ability	■		■	■	■	■			■
Accessiblity By Design				■		■			■
Advanced Wood Resources		■						■	
Aged Woods							■	■	
American Marazzi Tile							■	■	
American Olean							■	■	
Andek Corp.						■		■	
Boa-Franc							■	■	
Boen Hardwood Flooring 1							■	■	
Boiardi Products Corp.						■			■
Bruce Hardwood Floors/An Armstrong Co.							■	■	
Bruce Laminate Floors/An Armstrong Co.							■	■	
Canital Granite							■		
The Carpet and Rug Institute	■			■		■			
Ceilings & Interior Sys.	■		■	■	■	■		■	■
Central Lock and Hardware Supply Co.						■		■	
Circle Redmont						■			
Columbia Forest Products							■	■	
Comtex Industries							■	■	
Congoleum Corp.	■		■					■	
CPN, Inc.		■					■	■	■
Crossville Ceramics Co.							■	■	
Dakota Granite							■	■	
Dal-Tile Corp.							■	■	
Dalton Paradise Carpet	■			■					
Dependable Chemical Co.		■							
E&E Consumer Products		■						■	■
Forbo Industries							■	■	
Formica Corp.							■	■	
Gibco Services							■	■	
Glen Oak Lumber & Milling/Sales Dept.							■	■	
Harris-Tarkett, Inc.							■	■	
Hartco Flooring Co./An Armstrong Company							■	■	
Interceramic, USA							■	■	
Italian Trade Commission, Tile Center							■	■	
Kentucky Wood Floors							■	■	

See listing for Manufactures and Suppliers Index for address and phone information.

Flooring

COMPANY	cushioned flooring	floor leveling materials	glare-inhibiting matte finishes	low-cut pile (versus loop pile) carpeting (½" max. pile)	natural cork flooring	slip-resistant flooring surfaces	wear-resistant flooring	Local dealer/distributor	Factory-direct
Kepcor/SSI Tiles						■	■	■	■
Latco Products							■	■	■
LDBrinkman	■		■			■	■	■	
London Tile Co.							■	■	■
LTS Ceramics							■	■	
Mannington Mills	■		■	■		■	■	■	
Marquis Carpet Mills				■					■
Mayse Woodworking Co.							■		
Metropolitan Ceramics							■	■	
Myro, Inc.						■		■	■
National Oak Flooring Manufacturers Assn.							■	■	
Norwegian Wood							■	■	
Oregon Lumber Co.							■		■
PermaGrain Products							■	■	
Plaza Hardwood							■	■	■
Polymer Plastics Corp.	■					■		■	
Quality Woods							■		
Quarry Tile Co.			■				■	■	
Robbins Hardwood Flooring/An Armstrong Co.							■	■	
Rocktile Specialty Products						■	■	■	■
Sandy Pond Hardwoods							■	■	■
Satin Finish Hardwood Flooring							■	■	
Solnhofen Natural Stone						■		■	■
The Structural Slate Co.							■	■	■
Summitville Tiles						■	■	■	
Terra-Green Ceramics 2							■	■	
Texas Woods, Inc.						■	■		■
UniBoard Canada/(St-Laurent Div.)							■	■	
United States Ceramic Tile Co.							■	■	■
Universal Marble & Granite							■	■	
Vermont Marble Co.							■		
Walker & Zanger			■				■	■	
Westchester Marble & Granite							■	■	■
Wilsonart Intl.						■		■	

See listing for Manufactures and Suppliers Index for address and phone information.

[1]Awards: ADEX Award (Mutenye)
Consumer Digest Award (Oak Select)

[2]Award: CTDA Diamond Award—Disney Headquarters

Garage Doors, Openers & Accessories

COMPANY	PRODUCTS																					SALES	
	doors with integral venting to exterior	oversized doors (min. 8' tall)	parking guidance systems	remote-control openers with large push buttons																		Local dealer/distributor	Factory-direct
Access-Ability	■	■	■	■																			■
Accessiblity By Design	■	■	■																				■
Central Lock and Hardware Supply Co.				■																		■	
Exeter Technologies, Inc.[1]			■																			■	■
Martin Door Mfg.	■	■																				■	■
Napco Security Systems				■																		■	
Sections, Inc.		■																				■	
Smarthome.com			■																				■
Wayne-Dalton [2]		■		■																		■	
Windsor Door		■		■																		■	

See listing for Manufactures and Suppliers Index for address and phone information.

[1] Awards: Park-Zone
  "One of the 10-Best Auto Accessories of the Year (1998)"—*Motor Trend*
  "One of the Year's 10-Best Gift Giving Items of 1998"—*Microsoft*
  "1999 Innovations Award for Design and Engineering"—*CES*
  "One of the Year's Top Buys in Personal Technology"—*US News and World Report*
  "1998 Award of Excellence"—*duPont Registry*
  "One of the Editor's Top Picks for 1999 Home Electronics"—*Popular Home Automation*

[2] Chairman's Commendation for Product Safety Advancement—Consumer Product Safety Commission

Hardware

COMPANY	extra-clearance swing-away hinges	integral lighted locks	levered locksets	push-button locks	remote-control locks	structural mounting hardware (grab bars)											Local dealer/distributor	Factory-direct
Access-Ability	■	■	■	■	■													■
Accessiblity By Design	■		■															■
Alarm Lock Systems			■	■	■												■	
Architectural Products by Outwater	■																	■
Arrow Lock Mfg. Co.			■														■	
Brass Accents by Urfic			■														■	
Cardinal Homes, Inc.			■	■													■	
Central Lock and Hardware Supply Co.	■	■	■	■	■												■	
Hafele America	■			■													■	
H.B. Ives			■														■	
Jackson Medical Equipment	■																	■
JADO Bathroom & Hardware Mfg. Corp.			■															
Kolson	■		■	■													■	■
Modular Hardware			■															
National Mfg.				■													■	
Omnia Industries, Inc.			■														■	
Pemko Mfg. Co.	■																	
Preso-Matic Keyless Locks				■													■	■
R & D Equipment	■																■	■
Sibes Brass			■														■	
Smarthome.com				■	■													■
Strom Plumbing By Sign Of The Crab			■	■													■	
Truth Hardware			■														■	
Watercolors			■	■	■												■	■
Wingits, LLC/Fastening Technology						■											■	■
Yale Security Group			■	■	■												■	

See listing for Manufactures and Suppliers Index for address and phone information.

Heating, Ventilation & Air Conditioning

COMPANY	air-quality systems	audible-signal thermostats	easy-access filter service location	humidity-sensing exhaust fans	HVAC toilets	large print thermostats	programmable exhaust fans	zone control cevices	Local dealer/distributor	Factory-direct
Access-Ability		■	■	■		■	■			■
Accessibility By Design						■				■
Advanced Wood Resources								■	■	
ADVent Intl.					■				■	
Air Vent				■						
American ALDES Ventilation	■						■		■	
Bask Technologies								■	■	■
Beacon/Morris								■	■	
Broan-NuTone				■			■		■	
Butler Ventamatic Corp.	■			■					■	
Calorique Ltd.								■	■	■
Cool Attic	■			■					■	
Dietmeyer, Ward & Stroud								■		■
Easy Heat								■	■	
Electric Mirror								■	■	
ENERJEE								■	■	■
Enertel Controls		■							■	■
Enerzone Systems	■	■							■	■
Fan America	■								■	■
Friedrich Air Conditioning Co.								■	■	
Heat Controller	■								■	
Heatway								■	■	
Honeywell Home & Building Control	■	■	■	■		■	■			
Hoyme Mfg.	■									
Independent Living Aids, Inc.		■				■				■
IntelliNet		■				■			■	
ISTEC Corp.								■	■	■
Jackson Medical Equipment	■									■
Kool-O-Matic Corp.	■			■			■		■	■
Leviton								■		
Maxxon Corp./(formerly Gyp-Crete Corp.)								■		
Miami-Carey Ltd.				■			■		■	
Myson								■	■	
Nutech Energy Systems Inc.	■								■	
Patton Building Products			■						■	
PFG Industries								■		■

See listing for Manufactures and Suppliers Index for address and phone information.

Heating, Ventilation & Air Conditioning

COMPANY	air-quality systems	audible-signal thermostats	easy-access filter service location	humidity-sensing exhaust fans	HVAC toilets	large print thermostats	programmable exhaust fans	zone control devices												Local dealer/distributor	Factory-direct
PSG Controls, Inc.						■														■	
Radiant Technology								■												■	
Rehau								■												■	
Research Products	■																			■	
Rheem Mfg./Air Conditioning Div.			■																	■	
Slant/Fin Corp.								■												■	
Smarthome.com						■															■
Space-Ray Infrared Gas Heaters								■												■	
Spruce Environmental Technologies	■																			■	
SSHC, Inc.								■													■
Sun Tunnel Skylights	■																			■	■
SunStar Heating Products								■												■	
Titon Inc.	■																			■	■
Vanguard Industries								■												■	
White-Rodgers/Emerson Electric Co.	■					■														■	

See listing for Manufactures and Suppliers Index for address and phone information.

Landscaping & Outdoor Products

COMPANY	automated awnings	automated gates	automated patio canopies	dual-door curbside mail boxes	exterior lighting	exterior railing systems	gutter guards	high color- or tactile-contrast walk edging	integral ice-thaw systems	irrigation/sprinkler products	lawn mats/tracks for vehicles	mail-arrival indication devices	maintenance-free decking and fencing	path lighting	raised-planter beds	slip-resistant composite deck/patio surfaces	slip-resistant concrete, granite or masonry surfaces	Local dealer/distributor	Factory-direct
Accessiblity By Design				■			■	■							■				■
Acme Brick Co./IBP Grid System																	■	■	■
ALLMET Building Products	■		■										■					■	
Americana Bldg. Products By Hindman Mfg.	■		■															■	
Anchor Wall Systems															■			■	■
Andek Corp.																■	■	■	
Architectural Landscape Lighting					■													■	
Architectural Products by Outwater													■						■
Ardee Lighting					■													■	
Argee Corp.					■													■	
Bomanite Corp.																	■	■	
Brite Millwork													■					■	
Calorique Ltd.									■									■	■
Cardiff Industries	■																	■	■
Central Lock and Hardware Supply Co.				■			■				■							■	
CertainTeed Corp. Pipe & Plastics Group													■					■	
Craft-Bilt Mfg. Co.	■		■															■	
Dakota Granite																	■	■	
DEC-K-ING						■							■					■	■
Easy Heat									■									■	
Englert Inc.							■											■	
Flos USA					■													■	
General Shale Brick								■							■			■	
Hanover Lantern					■													■	
.hessamerica					■													■	
Hubbell Lighting					■													■	
Idaho Wood					■									■					■
Kaycan							■											■	
Kolson					■													■	■
L. B. Plastics							■						■		■			■	
Leviton Mfg.					■									■				■	
Moultrie Mfg.						■							■					■	
Newstamp Lighting Co.					■													■	■
Old Carolina Brick Co.								■							■			■	
Polymer Plastics Corp.																■	■	■	
R & D Equipment		■	■	■									■		■			■	■

See listing for Manufactures and Suppliers Index for address and phone information.

Landscaping & Outdoor Products

COMPANY	automated awnings	automated gates	automated patio canopies	dual-door curbside mail boxes	exterior lighting	exterior railing systems	gutter guards	high color- or tactile-contrast walk edging	integral ice-thaw systems	irrigation/sprinkler products	lawn mats/tracks for vehicles	mail-arrival indication devices	maintenance-free decking and fencing	path lighting	raised-planter beds	slip-resistant composite deck/patio surfaces	slip-resistant concrete, granite or masonry surfaces				Local dealer/distributor	Factory-direct
Rehau									■												■	
Roberts Step-Lite Systems					■																■	
Sitecraft Inc.															■							■
Smart Deck Systems						■							■									■
Smarthome.com												■										■
SNOC					■																■	■
Southland Spa & Sauna													■								■	■
Systematic Irrigation Controls										■											■	■
Texas Woods, Inc.													■									■
Thomas Lighting/Consumer Div.					■																■	
Timber Tech																■					■	
TIR Systems Ltd.					■																■	
Trex Company													■			■					■	
Uni-Group U.S.A.																	■				■	■
Vermont Marble Co.								■														
Walker & Zanger																	■				■	
Windsor Door		■											■								■	
WR Bonsal Co.																	■				■	

See listing for Manufactures and Suppliers Index for address and phone information.

Plumbing, Faucets & Fixtures

PRODUCTS

COMPANY	bathing faucets with anti-scald features	bathing faucets with pressure monitoring	bath sinks with cantilevered lip at front edge	bath sinks with drain mounted at rear	bathtubs with access opening	bathtubs with faucet location offset to entry side	bathtubs with integral cushioning	bathtubs with integral grab bars	bathtubs with integral lift	bathtubs with integral seat	curbless shower bases	elongated toilets	foot-pedal bath faucets	foot-pedal kitchen faucets	hand-held showers with push-button control	hot water dispensers	HVAC toilets	infrared/motion-sensing bath faucets	infrared/motion-sensing kitchen faucets	kitchen sinks with drain control mounted on front edge	kitchen sinks with drain mounted at rear	toilets with integral personal-hygiene system	lever-handle bath faucets with pull-out sprayer	lever-handle kitchen faucets with pull-out sprayer	multiple compartment kitchen sinks with offset drains
Access-Ability	■	■	■	■	■	■	■	■	■	■	■	■	■	■	■			■	■	■	■	■	■	■	■
Accessiblity By Design	■	■	■	■	■	■	■	■	■	■	■				■							■	■	■	■
Accurate Ind. Steambath and Sauna																									
Acriform				■			■			■															
ADVent Intl.																				■					
Alsons Corp.															■										
American Marble Industries/Kephaco Corp.					■				■	■															
American Plumber																									
Americh Corp.					■	■	■		■	■															
Anaheim Mfg. Co.																■									
AquaGlass	■	■					■		■	■					■										
AquaHealth Systems, Inc.																									
Areslux		■																							
Astracast																				■	■				
Barclay Products	■	■	■	■	■			■							■					■			■	■	
Bates & Bates			■	■																	■				
Bath Ease 1				■	■		■		■						■										
Bath-Tec Whirlpool Bath/Builder Sales				■	■		■		■																
Burgess Intl. Bath Fixtures			■																						
Cardinal Homes, Inc.				■	■	■		■		■	■				■					■	■		■	■	■
Central Brass	■	■																■	■				■	■	
Central Lock and Hardware Supply Co.															■			■	■				■	■	
Chicago Faucets	■												■	■				■	■				■	■	
Concinnity/(A Div. of IW Industries)	■	■																					■	■	
Coni Marble Mfg.			■																				■	■	
Crane Plumbing/Fiat Products	■	■					■			■															
Dornbracht USA	■	■																					■	■	
Eljer Plumbingware	■	■		■			■		■						■									■	■
Elkay Mfg. Co.																					■			■	
Everpure																									
Federal Home Products																					■				
Fiberez Bathware				■				■		■															
Franke Consumer Products/Kitchen Sys.																					■		■	■	■
Geberit Mfg.																		■				■			
Gemini Bath & Kitchen Products																								■	
General Ecology																									

See listing for Manufactures and Suppliers Index for address and phone information.

Plumbing, Faucets & Fixtures Continued

PRODUCTS SALES

one-piece kitchen sinks for roll-under applications	shallow bath sinks (7½" max.)	shallow kitchen sinks (7½" max.)	shower heads on adjustable "slide" bar	shower units with integral grab bars	shower units with integral seat	single-lever bar faucets	single-lever bath faucets	single-lever kitchen faucets	sink faucets with anti-scald features	sink faucets with pressure monitoring	taller toilets (17" min. to seat top)	water treatment systems	whirlpool tubs with controls offset on entry side	Local dealer/distributor	Factory-direct
■	■	■	■	■	■	■	■	■	■	■	■		■		■
■	■	■	■	■	■	■	■	■	■	■	■		■		■
													■	■	■
			■	■									■		
				■										■	
				■										■	
											■			■	
												■		■	
				■										■	
				■	■	■							■		
											■			■	
				■											
	■		■	■	■		■	■		■	■			■	
				■										■	
													■		■
													■	■	■
														■	■
■			■	■	■	■		■	■				■	■	
						■	■							■	
				■				■	■	■				■	
						■	■	■						■	
						■	■	■						■	
														■	■
	■		■	■	■		■	■			■			■	
		■				■	■	■							
			■	■		■	■	■	■		■		■		
						■								■	
											■			■	
														■	
			■	■									■	■	
						■	■	■						■	
														■	
	■		■			■	■	■	■					■	■
													■	■	■

See listing for Manufactures and Suppliers Index for address and phone information.

PRODUCTS

COMPANY	bathing faucets with anti-scald features	bathing faucets with pressure monitoring	bath sinks with cantilevered lip at front edge	bath sinks with drain mounted at rear	bathtubs with access opening	bathtubs with faucet location offset to entry side	bathtubs with integral cushioning	bathtubs with integral grab bars	bathtubs with integral lift	bathtubs with integral seat	curbless shower bases	elongated toilets	foot-pedal bath faucets	foot-pedal kitchen faucets	hand-held showers with push-button control	hot water dispensers	HVAC toilets	infrared/motion-sensing bath faucets	infrared/motion-sensing kitchen faucets	kitchen sinks with drain control mounted on front edge	kitchen sinks with drain mounted at rear	toilets with integral personal-hygiene system	lever-handle bath faucets with pull-out sprayer	lever-handle kitchen faucets with pull-out sprayer	multiple compartment kitchen sinks with offset drains
Gerber Plumbing Fixtures Corp.		■										■													
Great Lakes Plastics					■	■	■	■		■															
Harrington Brass Works 2	■	■													■			■	■				■	■	
H.B. Ives	■	■																					■	■	■
Jackson Medical Equipment																						■			
Jacuzzi Whirlpool Bath	■	■								■															
JADO Bathroom & Hardware Mfg. Corp.	■	■																					■	■	
Jason Intl.	■									■															
Jensen Medical																						■			
Just Mfg. Co.																		■			■			■	■
Kinetico																									
Kohler Co.	■	■	■	■	■	■	■	■		■	■	■	■					■			■				■
Kolson	■	■	■	■	■	■	■	■		■	■	■	■	■	■					■	■	■	■	■	■
KWC Faucets	■	■													■			■	■	■	■		■	■	■
Lasco Bathware/(A Div. of Tomkins Industries)		■				■		■		■					■										
Leonard Valve Co.	■	■																							
Lifetime Faucets																							■		
Lippert Corp.											■												■		■
Lubidet USA 3																						■			
Lyons Industries																							■		
MAAX					■	■	■	■		■															
Mansfield Plumbing Products							■	■		■		■													
Medically Yours													■			■									
Mirolin Industries					■			■				■													
Moen	■	■																						■	
MTI Whirlpools						■		■																	
North Star Water Conditioning																									
Omni Corp.																									
Opella	■	■																					■	■	
Paul Decorative Products	■	■																						■	
Pearl Baths	■					■		■																	
Pedal Valves, Inc. 4													■	■											
Price Pfister	■	■														■								■	
Pro-Flo Products																									
Rainsoft Water Treatment Systems																									
Rapetti Faucets/(A Div. of George Blotcher)	■																						■	■	

See listing for Manufactures and Suppliers Index for address and phone information.

Plumbing, Faucets & Fixtures Continued

See listing for Manufactures and Suppliers Index for address and phone information.

one-piece kitchen sinks for roll-under applications	shallow bath sinks (7½" max)	shallow kitchen sinks (7½" max.)	shower heads on adjustable "slide" bar	shower units with integral grab bars	shower units with integral seat	single-lever bar faucets	single-lever bath faucets	single-lever kitchen faucets	sink faucets with anti-scald features	sink faucets with pressure monitoring	taller toilets (17" min. to seat top)	water treatment systems	whirlpool tubs with controls offset on entry side	Local dealer/distributor	Factory-direct
			■				■	■	■		■			■	
														■	
			■			■	■	■	■	■				■	
			■											■	
												■			■
			■	■	■							■		■	
			■				■	■						■	
			■		■	■	■					■		■	
			■												
■	■	■					■	■		■				■	
												■			
■	■	■	■	■	■	■	■	■	■		■	■		■	
■	■	■	■	■	■	■	■	■	■	■	■			■	■
■	■	■	■		■	■	■	■	■					■	
				■	■							■		■	
			■											■	
							■	■						■	
	■				■									■	
														■	■
												■		■	
				■	■							■		■	
■		■										■		■	■
															■
				■	■							■		■	
												■		■	
											■				
											■			■	■
			■			■	■	■						■	
			■											■	
			■		■							■		■	
														■	■
							■	■						■	
											■			■	■
											■				
														■	

COMPANY	bathing faucets with anti-scald features	bathing faucets with pressure monitoring	bath sinks with cantilevered lip at front edge	bath sinks with drain mounted at rear	bathtubs with access opening	bathtubs with faucet location offset to entry side	bathtubs with integral cushioning	bathtubs with integral grab bars	bathtubs with integral lift	bathtubs with integral seat	curbless shower bases	elongated toilets	foot-pedal bath faucets	foot-pedal kitchen faucets	hand-held showers with push-button control	hot water dispensers	HVAC toilets	infrared/motion-sensing bath faucets	infrared/motion-sensing kitchen faucets	kitchen sinks with drain control mounted on front edge	kitchen sinks with drain mounted at rear	toilets with integral personal-hygiene system	lever-handle bath faucets with pull-out sprayer	lever-handle kitchen faucets with pull-out sprayer	multiple compartment kitchen sinks with offset drains
Regency Industries								■		■	■														
Republic Stainless Steel Sinks																					■				
Rohl	■	■																						■	
Rynone Mfg. Corp.				■																					
SafeTek Intl.								■		■					■										
SEPCO Industries	■	■																					■	■	
Southland Spa & Sauna				■				■			■														
Speakman Co./Mfg. Div. 5	■	■													■			■	■		■				
St. Thomas Classics	■	■		■						■													■	■	
St. Thomas Creations	■	■	■	■						■													■	■	
Sterling Plumbing Group	■	■						■		■	■	■									■			■	
Strom Plumbing By Sign Of The Crab	■	■													■								■		
Symmons Industries	■	■													■									■	
Systematic Irrigation Controls																									
TFI Corp./Avanté																									
Toto USA												■										■			
Vita Bath										■					■										
Watercolors	■	■	■	■	■	■	■	■		■	■	■	■	■	■			■	■	■	■	■	■	■	■
Watertech								■																	
Westendorf Whirlpool																									
Wilsonart Intl.				■																	■				

See listing for Manufactures and Suppliers Index for address and phone information.

Plumbing, Faucets & Fixtures Continued

	one-piece kitchen sinks for roll-under applications	shallow bath sinks (7½" max.)	shallow kitchen sinks (7½" max.)	shower heads on adjustable "slide" bar	shower units with integral grab bars	shower units with integral seat	single-lever bar faucets	single-lever bath faucets	single-lever kitchen faucets	sink faucets with anti-scald features	sink faucets with pressure monitoring	taller toilets (17" min. to seat top)	water treatment systems	whirlpool tubs with controls offset on entry side	Local dealer/distributor	Factory-direct
PRODUCTS → **SALES**																
					■	■								■		
															■	■
				■				■	■						■	■
		■													■	■
				■	■											■
				■	■	■	■	■	■	■	■					
													■		■	■
				■						■					■	
				■							■				■	
		■		■					■		■				■	
					■		■	■	■						■	
							■	■	■						■	
				■	■	■		■	■						■	
													■		■	■
		■						■	■						■	■
											■				■	
				■	■	■								■	■	
	■	■	■	■	■	■	■	■	■	■	■	■		■	■	■
													■			
													■			■
		■													■	

See listing for Manufactures and Suppliers Index for address and phone information.

[1] American Society on Aging 1991 (Model 854)
[2] Award: ADEX (Victorian Pullout Kitchen Faucet)
[3] Best New Product 1993—American Society on Aging
[4] Pedalworks™
    Best New Products by *Today's Homeowner* 1997
    Best of Show—Kitchen and Bath Institute 1999
[5] *Consumers Digest* Best Buy (Anystream 2000 showerhead)

Speciality Products

COMPANY	adjustable closet storage systems	automated closet storage systems	built-in ironing centers with controls at bottom of unit	ceiling track lift and transport systems	central vacuums with baseboard dustpan	elevators/dumbwaiters	grab bars dia. 1¼" to 1½" with min. 5 colors/finishing choices	remote-control fireplaces	stairlifts	Local dealer/distributor	Factory-direct
Access-Ability	■	■	■	■	■	■	■	■	■		■
Accessiblity By Design	■			■			■				■
Alsons Corp.							■			■	
Architectural Products by Outwater			■				■				■
Auton Motorized Systems						■					
Barclay Products							■			■	
Braun Elevator Co.						■			■		■
Broan-NuTone					■					■	
Bruno Independent Living Aids, Inc. 1									■	■	■
Cabinet Studio	■		■							■	■
Central Lock and Hardware Supply Co.	■	■	■		■		■			■	
CentralVac Intl.					■					■	■
Clever Solutions				■						■	■
Concinnity/(A Div. of IW Industries)							■			■	
Create-A-Bed, C.A.B.			■							■	■
Custom Wood Products	■									■	
Decora Systems	■									■	■
Delaware Industries			■							■	■
Empire Comfort Systems								■		■	
Feeny Mfg. Co.	■									■	■

See listing for Manufactures and Suppliers Index for address and phone information.

WAUPACA DUMBWAITER

A Waupaca dumbwaiter adds the touch of beauty and effortless living that makes your customers home truly distinctive, while adding to their personal convenience. It gives your customers the utmost in flexibility and helps prevent back injuries, falls, and spills. The residential dumbwaiters can be used to transfer groceries, packages, firewood, laundry, dishes, and garbage recyclables from level to level. For further information contact: Waupaca Elevator, Inc. 1050 So. Grider St. Appleton, WI 54914-4858 1-800-238-8739

PRODUCTS / SALES

COMPANY	adjustable closet storage systems	automated closet storage systems	built-in ironing centers with controls at bottom of unit	ceiling track lift and transport systems	central vacuums with baseboard dustpan	elevators/dumbwaiters	grab bars dia. 1¼" to 1½" with min. 5 colors/finishing choices	remote-control fireplaces	stairlifts	Local dealer/distributor	Factory-direct
Franklin Brass Mfg. Co.							▪			▪	
Frontier Access & Mobility									▪		▪
GINGER/GUSA							▪			▪	
Hafele America							▪			▪	
Heat-N-Glo Fireplace Products								▪		▪	
Hunter Technology								▪		▪	
IRON-A-WAY			▪							▪	▪
Jackson Medical Equipment									▪		▪
Jensen Medical				▪		▪	▪		▪		
Lee/Rowan Co./Building Products Div.	▪										
Lift Aid				▪						▪	▪
M & S Systems					▪					▪	
Matot						▪				▪	
Medically Yours									▪		▪
Modular Hardware							▪				
Monterey Shelf	▪									▪	▪
Napoleon Fireplaces (Wolf Steel)								▪		▪	
National Mfg.	▪									▪	
Noil Kolly Signature Cabinets	▪									▪	▪
Nelson Medical							▪		▪		▪
Otto Bock							▪			▪	▪
Patton Building Products					▪					▪	
Paul Decorative Products							▪			▪	
Pro Smart Inc.		▪									▪
SafeTek Intl.							▪			▪	
Space-Metrics	▪									▪	
Superior Fireplace Co.								▪		▪	
Temco Fireplace Products								▪		▪	
VACUFLO—H-P Products					▪					▪	
Vance Industries	▪									▪	
Vanguard Plastics Ltd.	▪									▪	
Vent-A-Hood					▪					▪	
Vermont Castings								▪		▪	
Waupaca Elevator Co.						▪				▪	
White Home Products	▪	▪								▪	▪
Windquest Cos.	▪									▪	
Wingits, LLC/Fastening Technology							▪			▪	▪
Wood Technology	▪		▪							▪	

See listing for Manufactures and Suppliers Index for address and phone information.

[1]Award: Wisconsin Society of Professional Engineers—
"Excellence in Engineering" or Life Enrichment Award
(Electra-Ride III stairlift)

Structural Systems

COMPANY	flexible/adaptable room enclosures	pre-formed ramping systems	universal design component systems	universal design manufactured homes	universal design modular homes	universal design recreational systems											Local dealer/distributor	Factory-direct
Access-Ability		■	■															■
Accessiblity By Design		■																■
ALLMET Building Products	■																■	
Anchor Wall Systems		■															■	■
Aqua Plunge/Aqua Plunge Div.						■											■	■
Artistic Enclosures	■																■	
Bennett Industries	■																■	
Cardinal Homes, Inc.					■												■	
Fleetwood Homes 1				■													■	
Four Seasons Sunrooms	■																■	
Frontier Access & Mobility		■																■
Gothic Arch Greenhouses	■																	
Hartford Conservatories	■																■	■
The Home Store					■													■
Jackson Medical Equipment		■																■
Jensen Medical		■																
Mason Corp.	■																	
Metals USA-National Mfg.	■																■	
Nana Wall Systems	■																	■
Omega Sunspaces	■																■	■
Pivitol Suspension Seating			■														■	■
Playworld Systems, Inc. 2						■											■	
RAS Industries/Life-time Pre-formed Millwork			■														■	
Rio Plastics						■											■	
Screenex Retractable Door Systems Mfg.	■																■	
Seating Innovations			■														■	■
Sun Room Designs, Inc.	■																■	■
SunPorch Structures	■																	■
Woodfold-Marco Mfg.	■																■	

See listing for Manufactures and Suppliers Index for address and phone information.

[1] Award: Best New Home Design (Life Stages Home)

[2] Selected to participate in exhibit celebrating Universal Design at the Cooper-Hewitt National Design Museum

Walls, Finishes & Insulation

COMPANY	adjustable/tiltable mirrors	automated defogging mirrors	corner protectors	insulating paint	interior railing systems	package pass-through components	package shelves for entries	sound-insulated drywall	sound insulation	Local dealer/distributor	Factory-direct
Accessiblity By Design			■						■		■
American Polysteel									■	■	
Andek Corp.				■						■	
Architectural Products by Outwater			■								■
Around The Corner			■							■	
Ceilings & Interior Sys. Construction Assn.								■	■	■	■
Central Lock and Hardware Supply Co.			■							■	
CertainTeed Corp./Insulation Group									■	■	
Electric Mirror		■								■	
Fypon							■			■	
Gibco Services									■	■	
GINGER/GUSA	■									■	
Meyer Enterprises/Insul-Tray									■		
Owens Corning									■	■	
Polymer Plastics Corp.								■		■	
Poly-Tak Protection Systems			■							■	
Robern	■									■	
Thermo-Vu Sunlite Industries		■								■	
Tri-Guards			■							■	
Wingits, LLC/Fastening Technology					■					■	■
Woodfold-Marco Mfg.						■				■	

See listing for Manufactures and Suppliers Index for address and phone information.

Windows & Glass

COMPANY	adaptable/adjustable screening systems	awning-style windows with single-action operation	casement windows with lower single lock lever operation	electric window operators	glare-inhibiting films	manual window opening aids	shading systems	sound-insulated glazing	Local dealer/distributor	Factory-direct
ABC Seamless Siding		■						■	■	■
Access-Ability			■							■
Accessiblity By Design		■		■						■
Almetco Building Products	■	■						■	■	■
Aloido/Window Div.	■	■							■	
American Architectural Manufacturers Assn.	■	■	■	■		■				
American Heritage Shutters						■				■
Andersen Windows	■	■	■						■	
A-Solution					■				■	
Bennett Industries						■			■	
Caradco	■	■						■	■	
Cardiff Industries						■			■	■
Cardinal Homes, Inc.		■							■	
CertainTeed Corp. Pipe & Plastics Group						■			■	
Champagne Industries	■	■	■		■	■		■	■	■
CPFilms Inc.					■				■	
Eagle Window & Door	■	■				■		■	■	
Engineered Profiles	■	■							■	
Fillmore Thomas & Co.	■	■							■	■
Folding Shutter Corp.						■			■	■
Gorell Enterprises	■	■						■	■	
Great Lakes Window	■	■							■	
H-Window Company	■					■		■	■	
Hartford Conservatories		■							■	■
Hayfield Window & Door Co.	■	■							■	
The Hess Mfg. Co.	■	■							■	
Hurd Millwork Co.	■	■	■					■	■	
Huron Window Corp.	■	■							■	■
Insulate Windows	■	■			■			■	■	
Kaycan	■	■							■	
Kolbe & Kolbe Millwork Co.		■			■			■	■	
Logcrafters Log & Timber Homes	■	■								■
Malta Wood Windows & Doors	■	■							■	
Metals USA-National Mfg.		■							■	
National Woodworks	■	■						■	■	
Northeast Window and Door Assn.	■	■	■	■		■		■		

See listing for Manufactures and Suppliers Index for address and phone information.

Windows & Glass

COMPANY	adaptable/adjustable screening systems	awning-style windows with single-action operation	casement windows with lower single lock lever operation	electric window operators	glare-inhibiting films	manual window opening aids	shading systems	sound-insulated glazing	Local dealer/distributor	Factory-direct
Owens Corning		■	■					■	■	
Peerless Products		■	■					■	■	
Phifer Wire Products							■		■	
Poly-Tak Protection Systems				■					■	
Roto Frank of America				■			■		■	
Screenex Retractable Door Systems Mfg.	■						■		■	
Smarthome.com				■			■			■
Soft-Lite Windows 1			■						■	
Sun Room Designs, Inc.		■							■	■
Thermoplast		■	■						■	
Thermo-Vu Sunlite Industries				■	■		■	■		
Truth Hardware				■					■	
Victor Sun Control		■							■	
WENCO of Iowa/		■	■						■	
Windsor Windows			■						■	
Woodfold-Marco Mfg.							■		■	

See listing for Manufactures and Suppliers Index for address and phone information.

1 1999 Energy Star Regional Partner of the Year

Universal Homes You Can Build

According to an article by Ron Mace (who coined the term "universal design") "The intent of the universal design concept is to simplify life for everyone by making more housing usable by more people at little or no extra cost. Universal design is an approach to design that incorporates products as well as building features and elements which, to the greatest extent possible, can be used by everyone. While accessible or adaptable design requirements are specified by codes or standards for only some buildings and are aimed at benefitting only some people (those with mobility limitations), the universal design concept targets all people of all ages, sizes and abilities and is applied to all buildings."

In response to repeated requests from plan buyers all over the country, Home Planners has joined forces with the experts at both the Center for Universal Design at North Carolina State University and The Philip Stephen Companies to develop a portfolio of stock blueprints for universal homes. Each of these homes has been carefully designed to include as many universal features as possible. They include, among other things, three specific issues that must be incorporated at the planning and designing stages: space planning for flexibility and future change; early planning of entrances and egresses; planning for appropriate products and the possibility of additional or new products in the future.

Universal homes all incorporate a variety of components, most of which are common throughout the designs shown on the following pages. Generally, it is important that steps be eliminated or configured so that gentle inclines, lifts and other maneuverability devices can be added. Entries need to be flush or nearly so, to avoid steps, as well. Wider hallways and doorways accommodate easier mobility, make moving day easier for everyone and simply add spaciousness and brightness to the floor plan.

Living areas are open, with no change in elevation from one area to another. Natural light fills many of the spaces, making them seem even more spacious.

Flexible-space bathrooms and kitchens are a must. Wide spaces in the kitchen with plenty of room to move about and the possibility of adjustable countertops, range tops and cabinetry allow for easy and convenient remodeling at a later time. The kitchen may also include such benefits as a sink and cooktop with open knee-space, an end-of-counter oven (or one with knee-space beside it) and possibly lowered eat-in counters. Baths (or at least the master) should include showers with seats, or curbless showers, and should be easily convertible for the addition of grab bars, side-load toilets and other convenient fixtures, if they are not installed at the building stage. Baths (or at least one bath in the plan) should feature plenty of maneuvering space and allow for easy access to all fixtures.

Closets (or at least a master-bedroom closet) should be large enough to move into and turn around in easily. Adjustable closet storage systems further add to their convenience.

Other amenities that are often found in the universal home are such things as mud rooms, computer or resource rooms, mother-in-law suites, and other flexible/adaptable spaces that meet immediate goals as well as future needs.

All of these universal features are designed to create the most flexible, livable space for the homeowner, both now and in the future. The homes encompass the finest in design, the most convenient layouts and, as the term "universal" implies, are intended to beautifully surround the homeowner, his friends and family with comfortable, convenient space. They consider such things as young children in the home, an aging parent in the home, and friends and family members who may have mobility considerations. Enabling accommodations are, in the best universal style, integral, invisible and efficient. The true joy of universal design is its ability to accommodate all lifestyles and needs, while maintaining aesthetics and convenience for all.

Browse through the homes on the following pages. They include everything from compact cottages to massive estates, in a wide range of styles. Once you've made a choice on a home you'd like to build, you can order complete construction drawings for that home. Just turn to the ordering pages 110-113 and you're on your way to fine universal design.

DESIGN HPT01001

Square Footage: 786

Price Tier: A1

- Open living areas
- Storage area and shower space flexible to accommodate various bath fixtures and configurations
- Covered porches front and rear
- Compact kitchen with open space under sink
- Folding work table surface adjacent to compact laundry

DESIGN BY
©The Philip Stephen Companies, Inc.

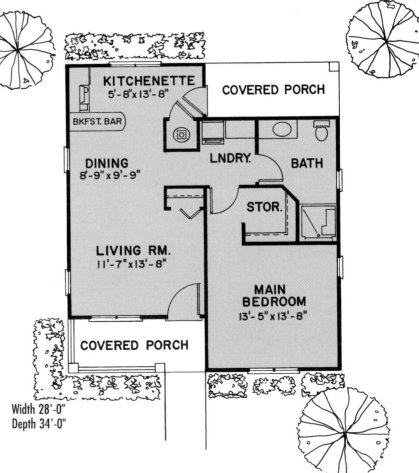

KITCHENETTE
5'-8"x13'-8"

COVERED PORCH

BKFST. BAR

DINING
8'-9"x9'-9"

LNDRY.

BATH

STOR.

LIVING RM.
11'-7"x13'-8"

MAIN BEDROOM
13'-5"x13'-8"

COVERED PORCH

Width 28'-0"
Depth 34'-0"

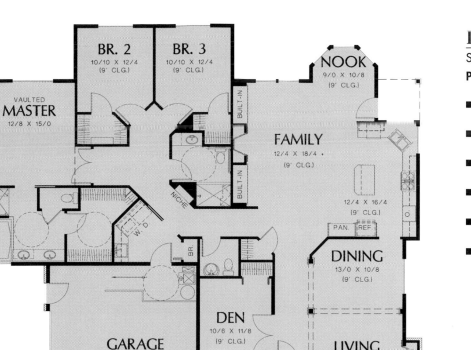

Floor plan labels:

VAULTED MASTER
12/8 X 15/0

BR. 2
10/10 X 12/4
(9' CLG.)

BR. 3
10/10 X 12/4
(9' CLG.)

NOOK
9/0 X 10/8
(9' CLG.)

FAMILY
12/4 X 18/4 +
(9' CLG.)

12/4 X 16/4
(9' CLG.)

DINING
13/0 X 10/8
(9' CLG.)

DEN
10/6 X 11/8
(9' CLG.)

GARAGE
21/0 X 24/6 +/-

LIVING
13/0 X 12/8
(9' CLG.)

BUILT-IN
NICHE
W D
PAN. REF.
BR

Width 63'-0"
Depth 60'-0"

DESIGN HPT01002

Square Footage: 2,394

Price Tier: A4

- Adaptable base cabinets in baths and kitchen
- Octagonal nook surrounded with glass
- Open living and dining rooms, defined by columns
- Vaulted owners suite with accessible private bath
- Walk-in closets in each bedroom
- Island kitchen with pantry

DESIGN BY
©Alan Mascord
Design Associates, Inc.

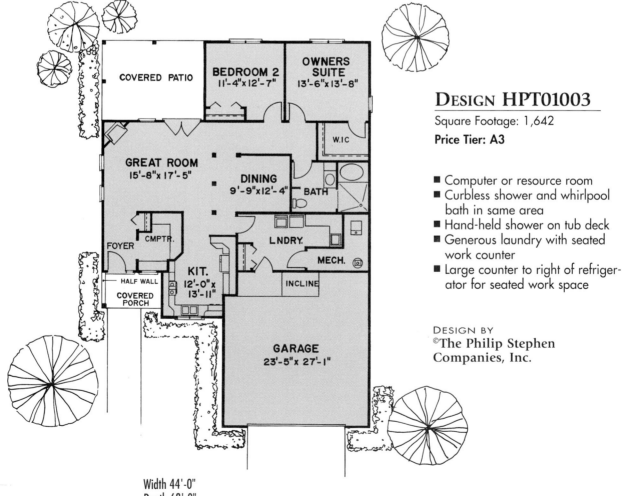

COVERED PATIO

BEDROOM 2
11'-4"x12'-7"

OWNERS SUITE
13'-6"x13'-8"

W.IC

GREAT ROOM
15'-8"x 17'-5"

DINING
9'-9"x12'-4"

BATH

FOYER

CMPTR.

LNDRY.

MECH.

HALF WALL

KIT.
12'-0"x
13'-11"

INCLINE

COVERED PORCH

GARAGE
23'-5"x 27'-1"

Width 44'-0"
Depth 68'-0"

Design HPT01003

Square Footage: 1,642

Price Tier: A3

- Computer or resource room
- Curbless shower and whirlpool bath in same area
- Hand-held shower on tub deck
- Generous laundry with seated work counter
- Large counter to right of refrigerator for seated work space

Design by
©The Philip Stephen Companies, Inc.

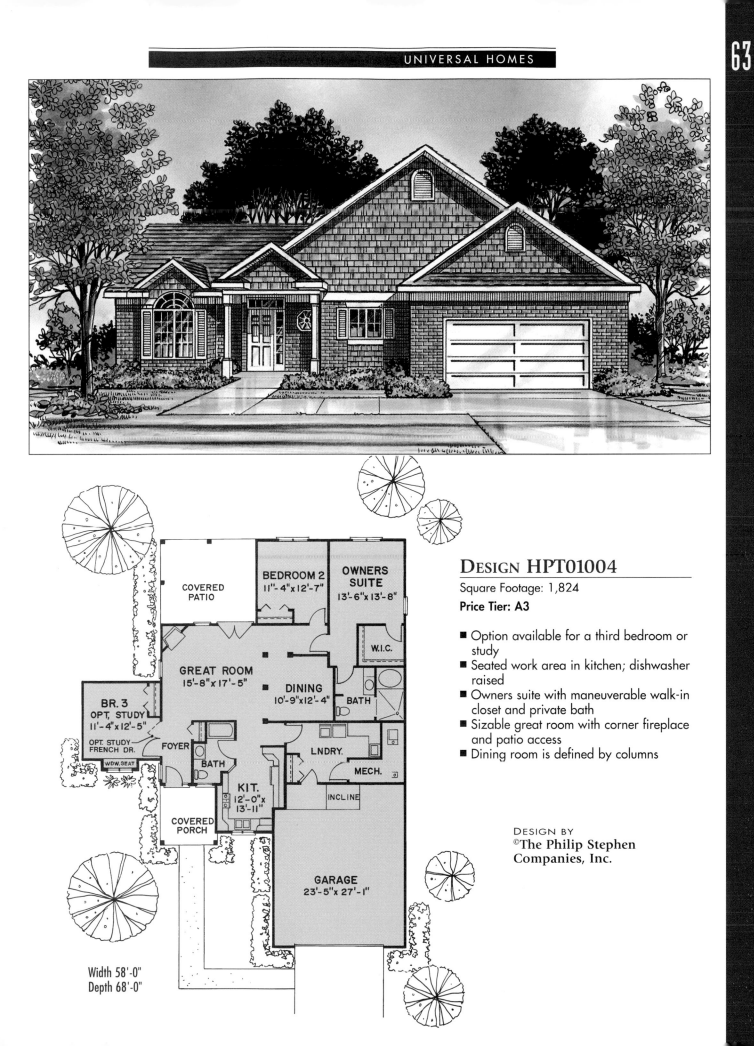

DESIGN HPT01004

Square Footage: 1,824

Price Tier: A3

- Option available for a third bedroom or study
- Seated work area in kitchen; dishwasher raised
- Owners suite with maneuverable walk-in closet and private bath
- Sizable great room with corner fireplace and patio access
- Dining room is defined by columns

DESIGN BY
©The Philip Stephen
Companies, Inc.

Floor plan labels:

COVERED PATIO

BEDROOM 2
11"-4"x12'-7"

OWNERS SUITE
13'-6"x13'-8"

W.I.C.

GREAT ROOM
15'-8"x17'-5"

DINING
10'-9"x12'-4"

BATH

BR. 3
OPT. STUDY
11'-4"x12'-5"

OPT. STUDY
FRENCH DR.

WDW. SEAT

FOYER

BATH

LNDRY.

MECH.

KIT.
12'-0"x
13'-11"

INCLINE

COVERED PORCH

GARAGE
23'-5"x27'-1"

Width 58'-0"
Depth 68'-0"

DESIGN HPT01005

Square Footage: 1,904

Price Tier: A3

- Three bedrooms include private owners suite
- Main bath features flexible closet and tub to accommodate varied fixtures
- Kitchen with pass-through counter
- Computer or resource room may be converted to elevator space when lower-level finished
- Each bath has easily maneuverable bathing and toilet areas.
- Two-car, side-load garage

DESIGN BY
©The Philip Stephen Companies, Inc.

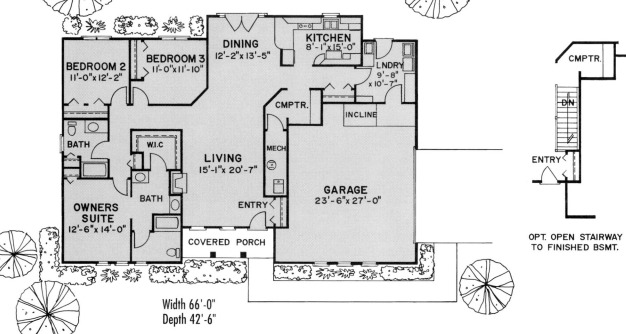

DINING
12'-2"x13'-5"

KITCHEN
8'-1"x15'-0"

BEDROOM 2
11'-0"x12'-2"

BEDROOM 3
11'-0"x11'-10"

LNDRY
9'-8"
x10'-7"

CMPTR.

BATH

W.I.C

LIVING
15'-1"x 20'-7"

MECH

INCLINE

OWNERS
SUITE
12'-6"x14'-0"

BATH

ENTRY

GARAGE
23'-6"x 27'-0"

COVERED PORCH

Width 66'-0"
Depth 42'-6"

CMPTR.

DN

ENTRY

OPT. OPEN STAIRWAY
TO FINISHED BSMT.

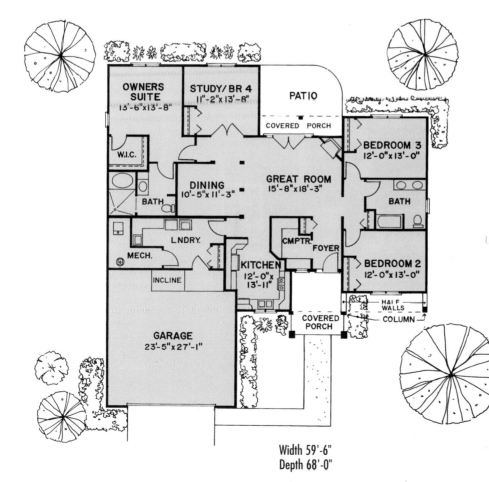

DESIGN HPT01006

Square Footage: 2,205

Price Tier: A4

- Owners suite and two (or three) family bedrooms
- Use Bedroom 4 as a study if preferred
- Open great room and formal dining room
- Laundry offers seated work counter
- Computer or resource room with window at entry
- Owners bath features skylit, curbless shower and whirlpool tub with hand-held shower on tub deck
- Counter in kitchen offers seated work space

Width 59'-6"
Depth 68'-0"

DESIGN BY
©The Philip Stephen
Companies, Inc.

DESIGN HPT01007

Square Footage: 1,870

Price Tier: A3

- Two- or three-bedroom design
- Study option opens with optional French door
- Computer or resource room and alcove
- Angular breakfast bar between kitchen and dining room
- Owners suite with double-door entry and private bath; seat in shower
- Open knee-space counters in kitchen, main bath and laundry

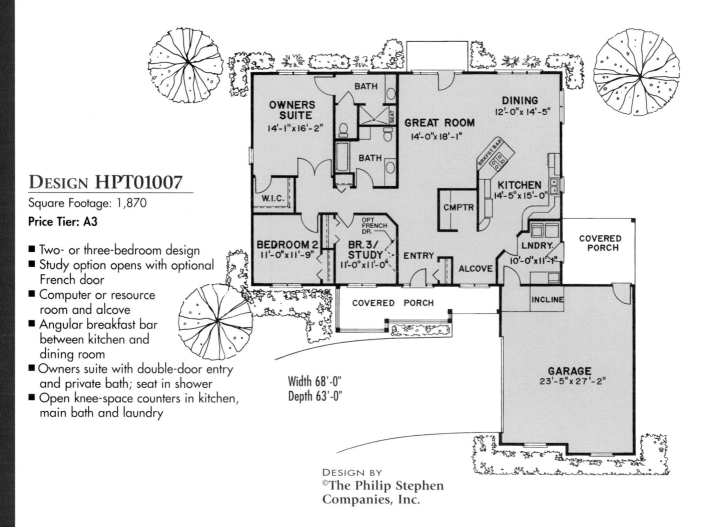

Width 68'-0"
Depth 63'-0"

DESIGN BY
©The Philip Stephen
Companies, Inc.

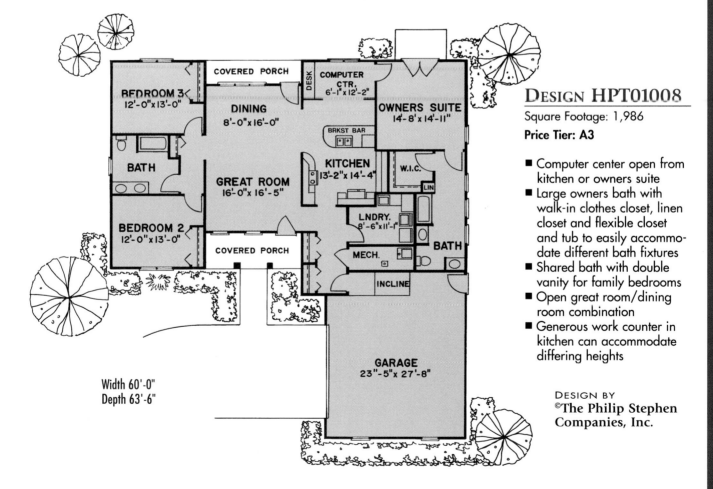

COVERED PORCH

BEDROOM 3
12'-0"x13'-0"

DINING
8'-0"x16'-0"

DESK

COMPUTER
CTR.
6'-1"x12'-2"

OWNERS SUITE
14-8'x14'-11"

BRKST BAR

KITCHEN
13'-2"x14'-4"

W.I.C.

BATH

GREAT ROOM
16'-0"x16'-5"

LIN

BEDROOM 2
12'-0"x13'-0"

LNDRY.
8'-6"x11'-1"

COVERED PORCH

MECH.

BATH

INCLINE

GARAGE
23"-5"x 27'-8"

Width 60'-0"
Depth 63'-6"

DESIGN HPT01008

Square Footage: 1,986

Price Tier: A3

- Computer center open from kitchen or owners suite
- Large owners bath with walk-in clothes closet, linen closet and flexible closet and tub to easily accommodate different bath fixtures
- Shared bath with double vanity for family bedrooms
- Open great room/dining room combination
- Generous work counter in kitchen can accommodate differing heights

DESIGN BY
©The Philip Stephen
Companies, Inc.

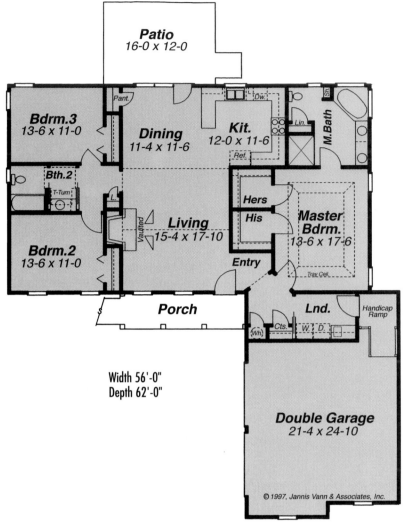

Patio
16-0 x 12-0

Bdrm.3
13-6 x 11-0

Pant.

Dining
11-4 x 11-6

Kit.
12-0 x 11-6

Dw.

Ref.

Lin.

Sh.

M.Bath

Bth.2

T-Turn

Hers

His

Living
15-4 x 17-10

Vaulted

Master Bdrm.
13-6 x 17-6

Bdrm.2
13-6 x 11-0

Entry

Trav. Ceil.

Porch

Lnd.

Handicap Ramp

Wh.

Cts.

W. D.

Width 56'-0"
Depth 62'-0"

Double Garage
21-4 x 24-10

© 1997, Jannis Vann & Associates, Inc.

Design HPT01009

Square Footage: 1,676

Price Tier: A3

- Living area with fireplace and adjoining dining room
- Flexible, maneuverable space in kitchen
- Compliant owners bath with full turning radius
- C-shaped kitchen with snack-bar counter
- Two family bedrooms with shared bath
- Covered porch and rear patio with flush entries

Design by
©Jannis Vann
& Associates, Inc.

©1999 Donald A. Gardner, Inc.

B.NATHAN

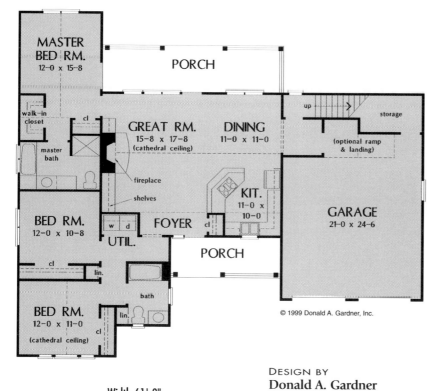

MASTER
BED RM.
12-0 x 15-8

walk-in
closet

cl

master
bath

PORCH

GREAT RM.
15-8 x 17-8
(cathedral ceiling)

DINING
11-0 x 11-0

up

storage

(optional ramp
& landing)

fireplace

shelves

KIT.
11-0 x
10-0

GARAGE
21-0 x 24-6

BED RM.
12-0 x 10-8

w d

FOYER

cl

UTIL.

PORCH

cl

lin.

bath

lin.

BED RM.
12-0 x 11-0
(cathedral ceiling)

cl

© 1999 Donald A. Gardner, Inc.

Width 61'-0"
Depth 51'-8"

DESIGN BY
Donald A. Gardner
Architects, Inc.

DESIGN HPT01010

Square Footage: 1,425

Price Tier: A2

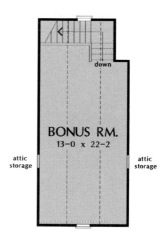

down

BONUS RM.
13-0 x 22-2

attic
storage

attic
storage

- Cathedral ceilings in great room, master bedroom and one family bedroom
- Open dining/great room/kitchen area
- Walk-in closet in owners bedroom; owners bath with oversized shower
- Large storage area in garage
- Covered porches front and rear

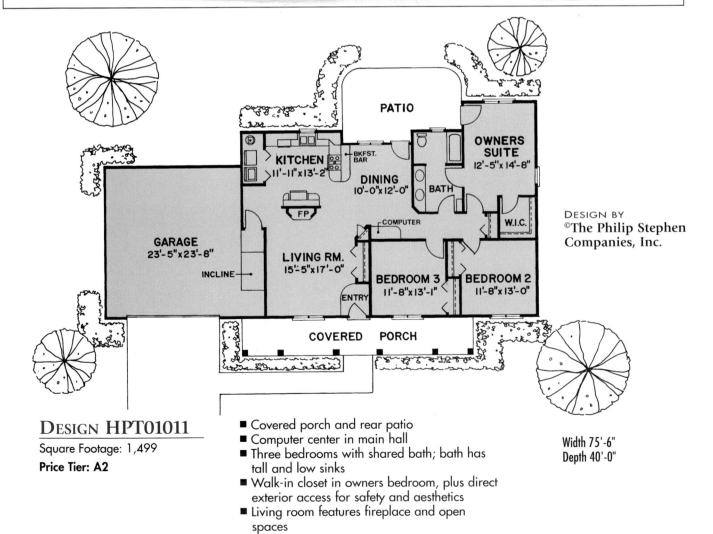

DESIGN HPT01011

Square Footage: 1,499

Price Tier: A2

- Covered porch and rear patio
- Computer center in main hall
- Three bedrooms with shared bath; bath has tall and low sinks
- Walk-in closet in owners bedroom, plus direct exterior access for safety and aesthetics
- Living room features fireplace and open spaces

DESIGN BY
©The Philip Stephen Companies, Inc.

Width 75'-6"
Depth 40'-0"

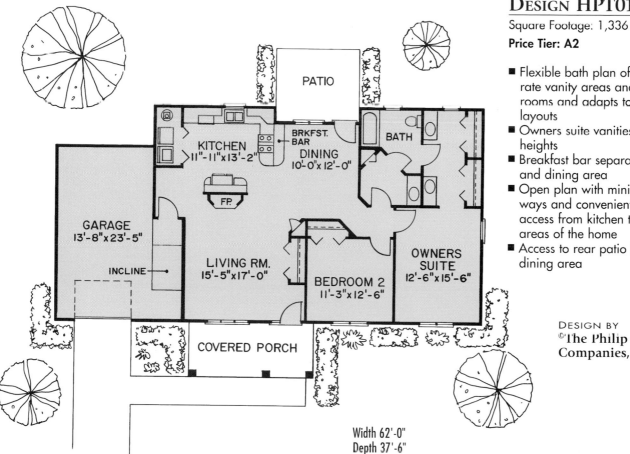

PATIO

KITCHEN
11"-11"x13'-2"

BRKFST.
BAR

DINING
10'-0"x12'-0"

BATH

FP.

GARAGE
13'-8"x23'-5"

INCLINE →

LIVING RM.
15'-5"x17'-0"

BEDROOM 2
11'-3"x12'-6"

OWNERS
SUITE
12'-6"x15'-6"

COVERED PORCH

Width 62'-0"
Depth 37'-6"

DESIGN HPT01012

Square Footage: 1,336
Price Tier: A2

- Flexible bath plan offers separate vanity areas and dressing rooms and adapts to future layouts
- Owners suite vanities at varying heights
- Breakfast bar separates kitchen and dining area
- Open plan with minimal hallways and convenient visual access from kitchen to most areas of the home
- Access to rear patio from dining area

DESIGN BY
©The Philip Stephen
Companies, Inc.

DESIGN HPT01013

Square Footage: 1,864

Price Tier: A3

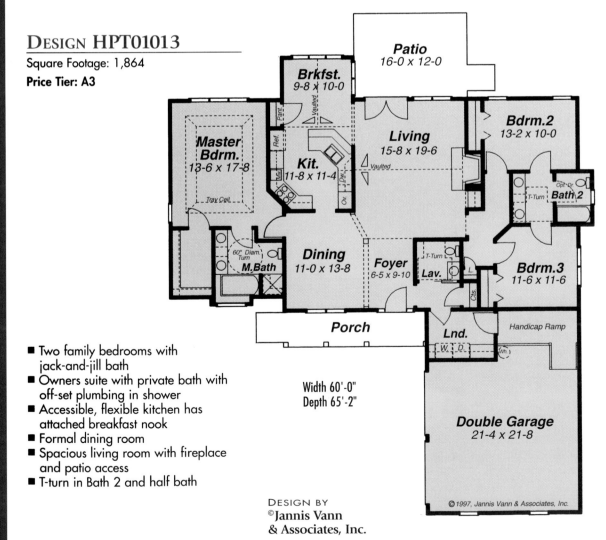

Width 60'-0"
Depth 65'-2"

- Two family bedrooms with jack-and-jill bath
- Owners suite with private bath with off-set plumbing in shower
- Accessible, flexible kitchen has attached breakfast nook
- Formal dining room
- Spacious living room with fireplace and patio access
- T-turn in Bath 2 and half bath

DESIGN BY
©Jannis Vann
& Associates, Inc.

©1997, Jannis Vann & Associates, Inc.

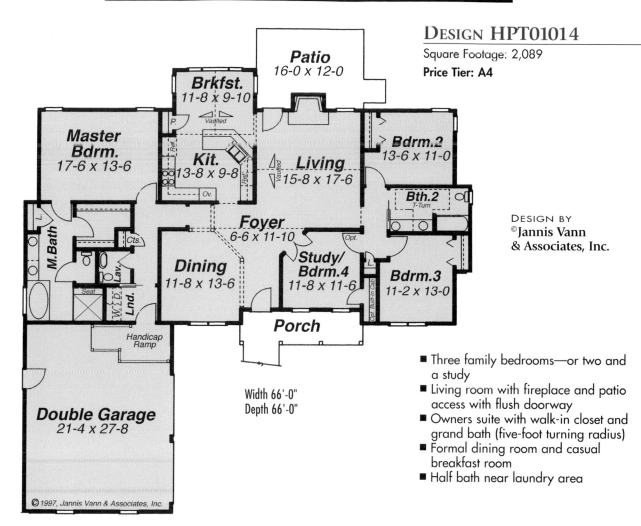

Patio
16-0 x 12-0

Brkfst.
11-8 x 9-10

Vaulted

Master Bdrm.
17-6 x 13-6

Kit.
13-8 x 9-8

Living
15-8 x 17-6

Vaulted

Bdrm.2
13-6 x 11-0

Bth.2
T-Turn

M. Bath

Cts.

Foyer
6-6 x 11-10

Opt.

Dining
11-8 x 13-6

Study/ Bdrm.4
11-8 x 11-6

Bdrm.3
11-2 x 13-0

Seat

W/D/ Lav. Lnd.

Opt. Built-In Cab.

Porch

Handicap Ramp

Double Garage
21-4 x 27-8

© 1997, Jannis Vann & Associates, Inc.

Width 66'-0"
Depth 66'-0"

DESIGN HPT01014

Square Footage: 2,089

Price Tier: A4

DESIGN BY
©Jannis Vann
& Associates, Inc.

- Three family bedrooms—or two and a study
- Living room with fireplace and patio access with flush doorway
- Owners suite with walk-in closet and grand bath (five-foot turning radius)
- Formal dining room and casual breakfast room
- Half bath near laundry area

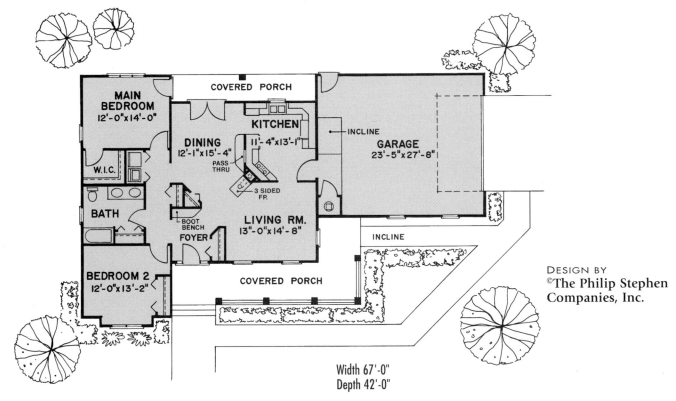

Width 67'-0"
Depth 42'-0"

DESIGN BY
©The Philip Stephen
Companies, Inc.

DESIGN HPT01015

Square Footage: 1,269

Price Tier: A2

- Wrapping front porch with stairs and gentle incline
- Boot bench and coat closet in entry
- Shared bath with double vanities
- Three-sided fireplace between living and dining rooms
- Pass-through counter separates kitchen and dining room

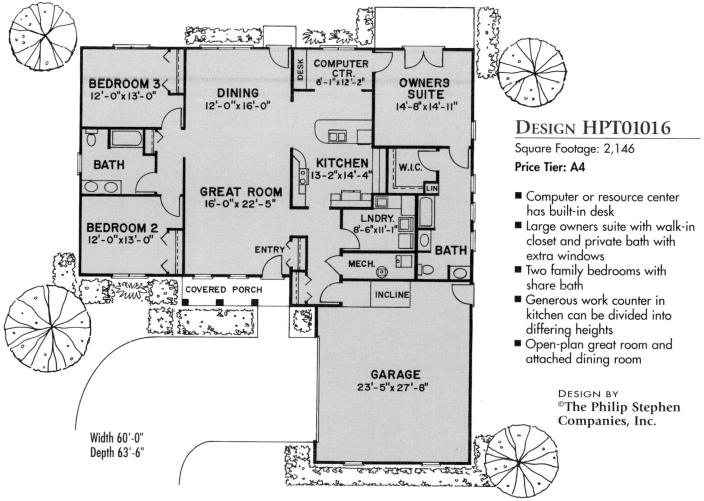

BEDROOM 3
12'-0"x13'-0"

DINING
12'-0"x16'-0"

DESK

COMPUTER CTR.
8'-1"x12'-2"

OWNERS SUITE
14'-8"x14'-11"

BATH

KITCHEN
13'-2"x14'-4"

W.I.C.

LIN

GREAT ROOM
16'-0"x22'-5"

LNDRY.
8'-6"x11'-1"

BEDROOM 2
12'-0"x13'-0"

ENTRY

MECH.

BATH

COVERED PORCH

INCLINE

GARAGE
23'-5"x27'-8"

Width 60'-0"
Depth 63'-6"

Design HPT01016

Square Footage: 2,146

Price Tier: A4

- Computer or resource center has built-in desk
- Large owners suite with walk-in closet and private bath with extra windows
- Two family bedrooms with share bath
- Generous work counter in kitchen can be divided into differing heights
- Open-plan great room and attached dining room

DESIGN BY
©The Philip Stephen
Companies, Inc.

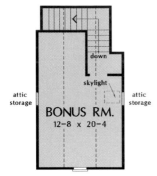

attic storage

down

skylight

attic storage

BONUS RM.
12-8 x 20-4

DESIGN BY
Donald A. Gardner
Architects, Inc.

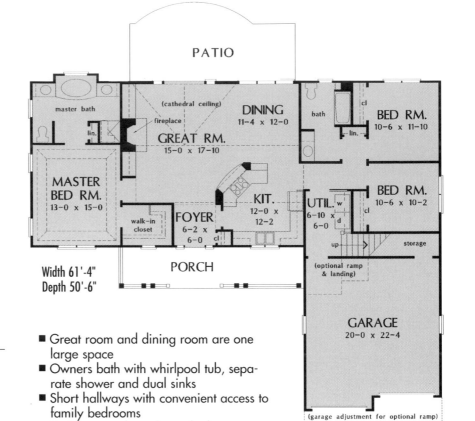

PATIO

master bath

(cathedral ceiling)

DINING
11-4 x 12-0

bath

cl

BED RM.
10-6 x 11-10

lin.

fireplace

lin.

GREAT RM.
15-0 x 17-10

MASTER
BED RM.
13-0 x 15-0

KIT.
12-0 x
12-2

UTIL.
6-10 x
6-0

w
d

cl

BED RM.
10-6 x 10-2

walk-in
closet

FOYER
6-2 x
6-0

cl

up

storage

(optional ramp
& landing)

Width 61'-4"
Depth 50'-6"

PORCH

GARAGE
20-0 x 22-4

(garage adjustment for optional ramp)

© 1999 Donald A. Gardner, Inc.

DESIGN HPT01017

Square Footage: 1,601

Price Tier: A3

- Great room and dining room are one large space
- Owners bath with whirlpool tub, separate shower and dual sinks
- Short hallways with convenient access to family bedrooms
- Kitchen pass-through overlooks great room
- Two-car garage with storage area

©1999 Donald A. Gardner, Inc.

©1999 Donald A. Gardner, Inc.

B.NATHAN

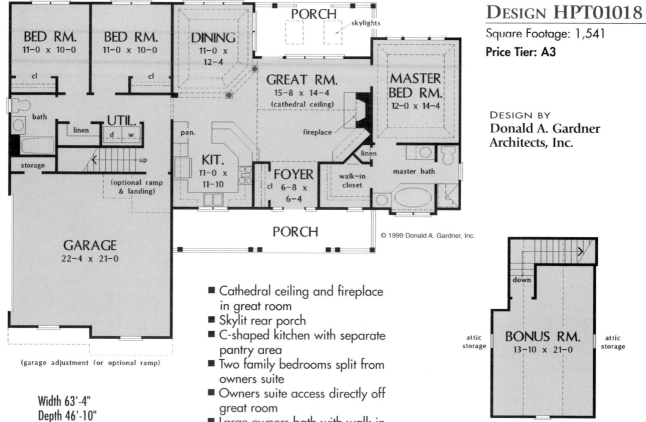

BED RM.
11-0 x 10-0

BED RM.
11-0 x 10-0

DINING
11-0 x 12-4

PORCH

skylights

GREAT RM.
15-8 x 14-4
(cathedral ceiling)

MASTER BED RM.
12-0 x 14-4

cl

cl

bath

UTIL.
d   w

linen

pan.

fireplace

storage

up

(optional ramp & landing)

KIT.
11-0 x 11-10

FOYER
cl 6-8 x 6-4

linen

walk-in closet

master bath

GARAGE
22-4 x 21-0

PORCH

© 1999 Donald A. Gardner, Inc.

(garage adjustment for optional ramp)

Width 63'-4"
Depth 46'-10"

DESIGN HPT01018

Square Footage: 1,541

Price Tier: A3

DESIGN BY
**Donald A. Gardner
Architects, Inc.**

down

attic storage

BONUS RM.
13-10 x 21-0

attic storage

- Cathedral ceiling and fireplace in great room
- Skylit rear porch
- C-shaped kitchen with separate pantry area
- Two family bedrooms split from owners suite
- Owners suite access directly off great room
- Large owners bath with walk-in closet
- Utility room near an oversized linen closet

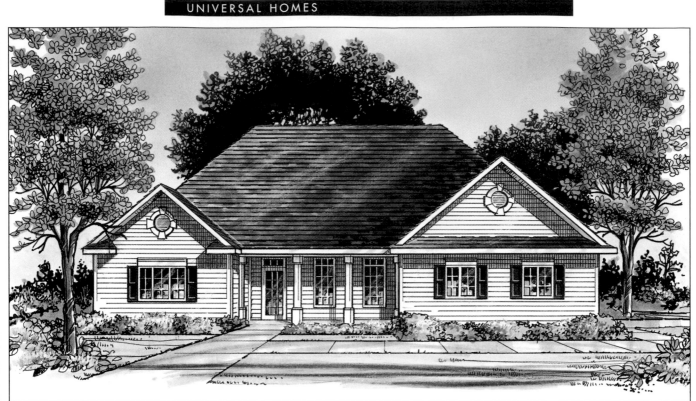

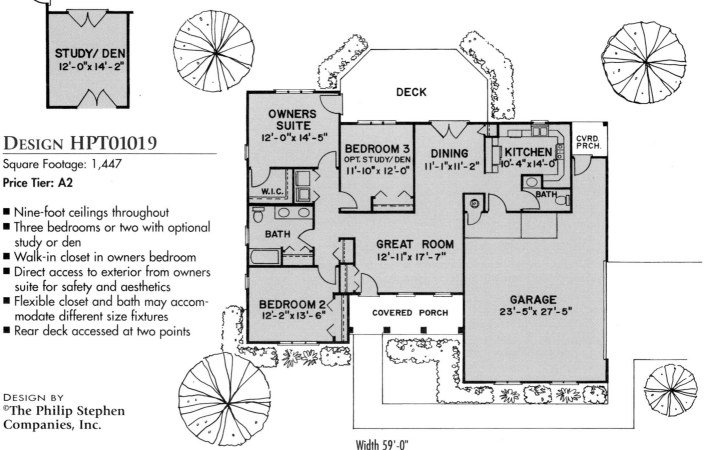

STUDY/ DEN
12'-0"x 14'-2"

Design HPT01019

Square Footage: 1,447

Price Tier: A2

- Nine-foot ceilings throughout
- Three bedrooms or two with optional study or den
- Walk-in closet in owners bedroom
- Direct access to exterior from owners suite for safety and aesthetics
- Flexible closet and bath may accommodate different size fixtures
- Rear deck accessed at two points

Design by
©The Philip Stephen
Companies, Inc.

DECK

OWNERS SUITE
12'-0"x 14'-5"

W.I.C.

BATH

BEDROOM 3
OPT. STUDY/ DEN
11'-10"x 12'-0"

DINING
11'-1"x11'-2"

KITCHEN
10'-4"x 14'-0"

CVRD. PRCH.

BATH

GREAT ROOM
12'-11"x 17'-7"

BEDROOM 2
12'-2"x13'-6"

COVERED PORCH

GARAGE
23'-5"x 27'-5"

Width 59'-0"
Depth 47'-6"

DESIGN HPT01020

Square Footage: 1,462

Price Tier: A2

DESIGN BY
©**The Philip Stephen
Companies, Inc.**

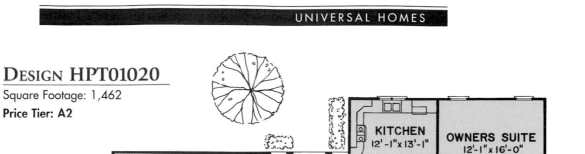

KITCHEN
12'-1"x 13'-1"

OWNERS SUITE
12'-1" x 16'-0"

BKFST. BAR

BREEZEWAY
12'-0"x 16'-0"

DINING
10'-8"x 15'-8"

W.I.C

GARAGE
23'-5" x 23'-5"

BATH

DESK

LIVING RM.
15'-8"x 16'-0"

CAB
SKYLITE
RESOURCE

BEDROOM 2
12'-0"x 13'-5"

- Breakfast bar separates kitchen and dining area
- Resource room with natural light
- Hand-held shower on tub deck; dual doors in bath; doorless dressing area
- Curbless shower and whirlpool in same area
- Stepless breezeway for access between garage, home and front or back yard

Width 66'-0"
Depth 53'-0"

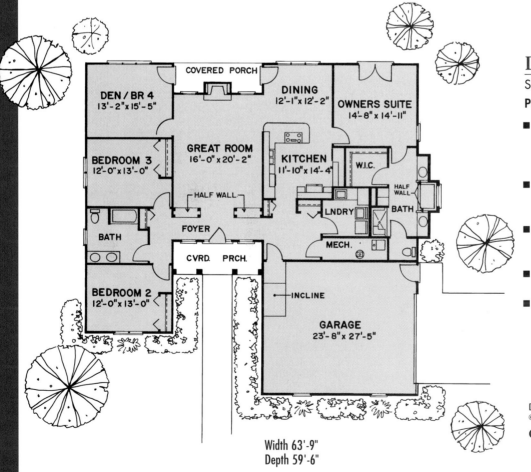

DESIGN HPT01021

Square Footage: 2,245

Price Tier: A4

- Portions of laundry may be combined with kitchen or owner's bath for modifications
- L-shaped kitchen with snack-bar counter through to dining room
- Owners suite and private bath on the right opens directly to exterior
- Three family bedrooms or two and a den on the left
- Walk-in closet in owners bedroom

DESIGN BY
©The Philip Stephen
Companies, Inc.

Width 63'-9"
Depth 59'-6"

Design IIPT01022

Square Footage: 2,285

Price Tier: A4

- Open dormer above entry
- Four bedrooms (or three and den) and two full baths
- Lavish owners bath with separate whirlpool tub and curbless shower, plus a walk-in closet with great maneuvering space
- Optional French doors in den
- Laundry offers seated work counter and allows space for future enhancements to the bath

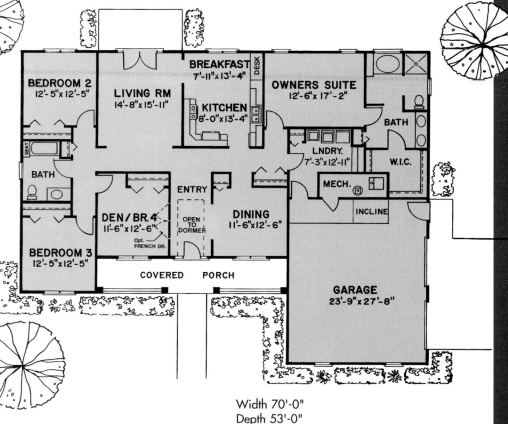

BREAKFAST
7'-11"x13'-4"

DESK

OWNERS SUITE
12'-6"x 17'-2"

BEDROOM 2
12'-5"x 12'-5"

LIVING RM
14'-8"x15'-11"

KITCHEN
8'-0"x13'-4"

BATH

LNDRY.
7'-3"x12'-11"

W.I.C.

SEAT

BATH

MECH.

INCLINE

ENTRY

DEN / BR. 4
11'-6"x 12'-6"

OPEN TO DORMER

DINING
11'-6"x12'-6"

Opt. FRENCH DR.

BEDROOM 3
12'-5"x12'-5"

COVERED   PORCH

GARAGE
23'-9"x 27'-8"

Width 70'-0"
Depth 53'-0"

DESIGN BY
©The Philip Stephen Companies, Inc.

DESIGN HPT01023

Square Footage: 1,921

Price Tier: A3

- Central great room defined by columns, half walls, fireplace and French doors to covered patio
- Kitchen with breakfast table and space for rolling cart adjoins dining room with porch access
- Luxury owners suite with French doors leading directly to yard
- Easy-access tub and shower, dual-height sinks and walk-in closet in owners bath
- Fold-down table in laundry area

DESIGN BY
©The Philip Stephen Companies, Inc.

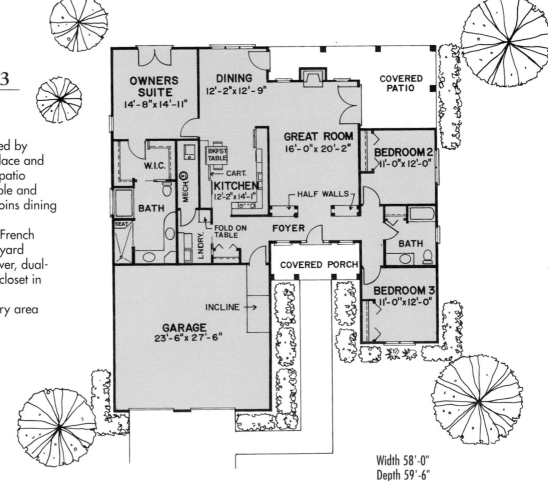

OWNERS SUITE 14'-8"x14'-11"

DINING 12'-2"x12'-9"

COVERED PATIO

W.I.C.

BKFST TABLE

GREAT ROOM 16'-0"x 20'-2"

BEDROOM 2 11'-0"x 12'-0"

BATH

MECH

CART.

KITCHEN 12'-2"x14'-1"

HALF WALLS

SEAT

LNDRY.

FOLD ON TABLE

FOYER

BATH

COVERED PORCH

INCLINE →

BEDROOM 3 11'-0"x12'-0"

GARAGE 23'-6"x 27'-6"

Width 58'-0"
Depth 59'-6"

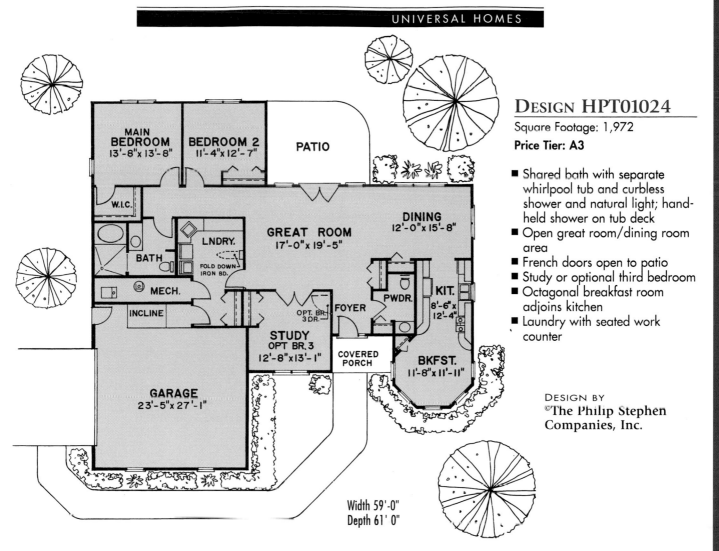

MAIN BEDROOM
13'-8"x 13'-8"

BEDROOM 2
11'-4"x 12'-7"

PATIO

W.I.C.

LNDRY.

GREAT ROOM
17'-0"x 19'-5"

DINING
12'-0"x 15'-8"

BATH

FOLD DOWN IRON BD.

MECH.

INCLINE

OPT. BR. 3 DR.

FOYER

PWDR.

KIT.
8'-6" x 12'-4"

STUDY
OPT BR. 3
12'-8"x13'-1"

COVERED PORCH

BKFST.
11'-8"x 11'-11"

GARAGE
23'-5"x 27'-1"

Width 59'-0"
Depth 61' 0"

DESIGN HPT01024

Square Footage: 1,972

Price Tier: A3

- Shared bath with separate whirlpool tub and curbless shower and natural light; hand-held shower on tub deck
- Open great room/dining room area
- French doors open to patio
- Study or optional third bedroom
- Octagonal breakfast room adjoins kitchen
- Laundry with seated work counter

DESIGN BY
©The Philip Stephen Companies, Inc.

DESIGN HPT01025

Square Footage: 1,743

Price Tier: A3

- Computer or resource room with built-in desk
- French doors in owners bedroom lead to rear yard
- Large open counter in kitchen for seated work space and convenient rolling cart space
- Two full baths; one with seat at tub foot
- Future adaptations made easy by combining part of laundry with kitchen or master bath
- Open plan eliminates halls and offers flexibility and maneuverability

DESIGN BY
©The Philip Stephen
Companies, Inc.

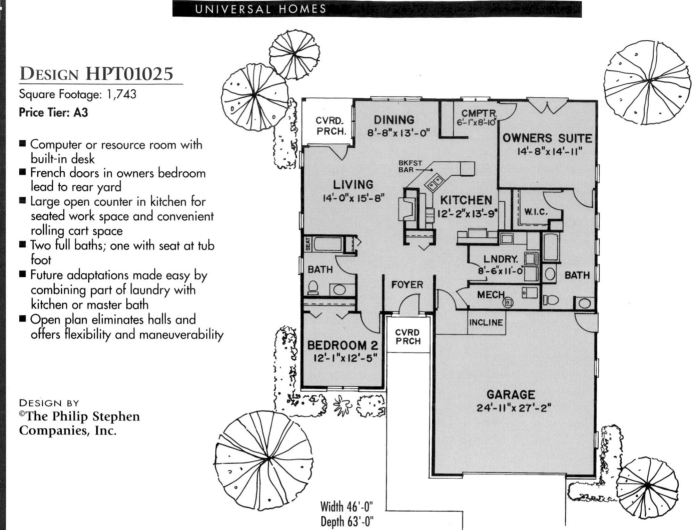

Width 46'-0"
Depth 63'-0"

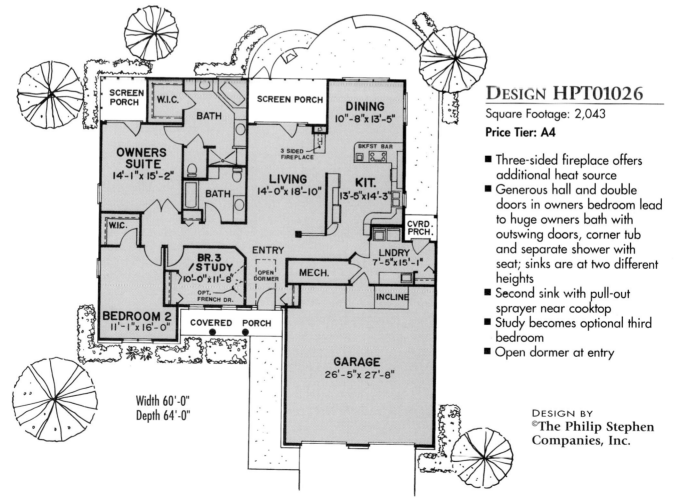

SCREEN PORCH

W.I.C.

BATH

OWNERS SUITE
14'-1" x 15'-2"

W.I.C.

SCREEN PORCH

DINING
10"-8" x 13'-5"

BKFST BAR

3 SIDED FIREPLACE

LIVING
14'-0" x 18'-10"

KIT.
13'-5" x 14'-3"

BATH

CVRD. PRCH.

BR. 3 /STUDY
10'-0" x 11'-8"

ENTRY

OPEN DORMER

OPT. FRENCH DR.

MECH.

LNDRY
7'-5" x 15'-1"

INCLINE

BEDROOM 2
11'-1" x 16'-0"

COVERED PORCH

GARAGE
26'-5" x 27'-8"

Width 60'-0"
Depth 64'-0"

DESIGN HPT01026

Square Footage: 2,043

Price Tier: A4

- Three-sided fireplace offers additional heat source
- Generous hall and double doors in owners bedroom lead to huge owners bath with outswing doors, corner tub and separate shower with seat; sinks are at two different heights
- Second sink with pull-out sprayer near cooktop
- Study becomes optional third bedroom
- Open dormer at entry

DESIGN BY
©The Philip Stephen Companies, Inc.

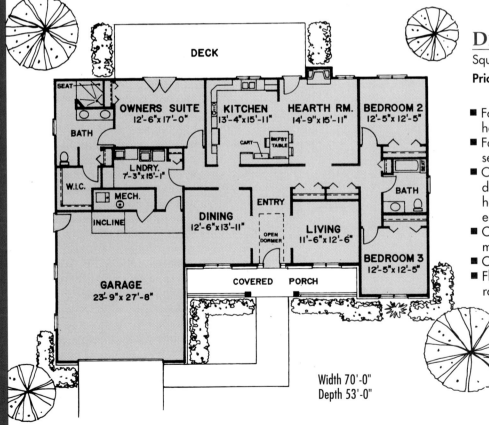

DECK

SEAT

OWNERS SUITE
12'-6"x17'-0"

KITCHEN
13'-4"x15'-11"

HEARTH RM.
14'-9"x15'-11"

BEDROOM 2
12'-5"x12'-5"

BATH

CART

BKFST
TABLE

LNDRY.
7'-3"x15'-1"

W.I.C.

MECH.

BATH

INCLINE

DINING
12'-6"x13'-11"

ENTRY

LIVING
11'-6"x12'-6"

OPEN
DORMER

BEDROOM 3
12'-5"x12'-5"

GARAGE
23'-9"x27'-8"

COVERED   PORCH

Width 70'-0"
Depth 53'-0"

DESIGN HPT01027

Square Footage: 2,295

Price Tier: A4

- Formal living and dining rooms, plus hearth room
- Family bedrooms share full bath that separates them
- Owners suite accesses rear deck through double doors and has bath with dual-height vanities, and an oversized shower with natural light
- Closet next to shower can accommodate motorized lift or spa equipment
- Open dormer above entry
- Flexible table space and area for a rolling cart in L-shaped kitchen

DESIGN BY
©The Philip Stephen
Companies, Inc.

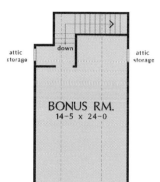

BONUS RM.
14-5 x 24-0

attic storage

down

attic storage

DESIGN BY
Donald A. Gardner
Architects, Inc.

- Hallways virtually eliminated for easy access
- Full master suite with two walk-in closets and maneuverable bath
- Utility room and mud room directly off kitchen
- Fireplace and built-ins in great room
- Three covered porches
- Storage in two-car garage

DESIGN HPT01028

Square Footage: 1,968

Price Tier: A3

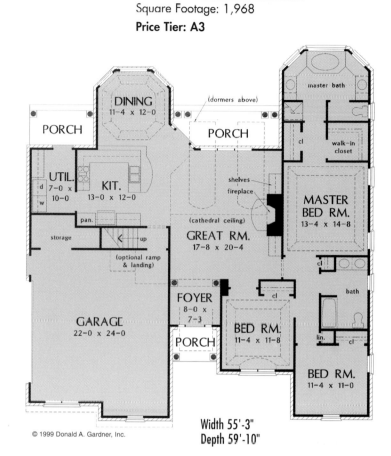

PORCH

DINING
11-4 x 12-0

(dormers above)

PORCH

master bath

cl

walk-in closet

UTIL.
7-0 x 10-0

d
w

KIT.
13-0 x 12-0

shelves
fireplace

MASTER BED RM.
13-4 x 14-8

pan.

storage

up

(optional ramp & landing)

(cathedral ceiling)

GREAT RM.
17-8 x 20-4

cl

cl

bath

FOYER
8-0 x 7-3

cl

BED RM.
11-4 x 11-8

lin.

cl

GARAGE
22-0 x 24-0

PORCH

BED RM.
11-4 x 11-0

© 1999 Donald A. Gardner, Inc.

Width 55'-3"
Depth 59'-10"

B. NATHAN

©1999 Donald A. Gardner, Inc.

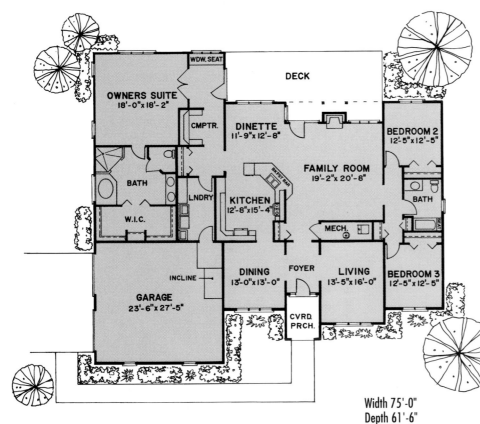

- Computer center
- Owners suite bath with separate curbless shower and whirlpool tub, dual sinks and maneuverable walk-in closet
- Full bath separates two family bedrooms
- Family room, dinette and kitchen form one large casual area
- Kitchen offers seated work space and rolling cart parking location
- Laundry may be combined with kitchen or owner's bath for future modifications

DESIGN BY
©The Philip Stephen Companies, Inc.

Width 75'-0"
Depth 61'-6"

DESIGN HPT01029

Square Footage: 2,940

Price Tier: C1

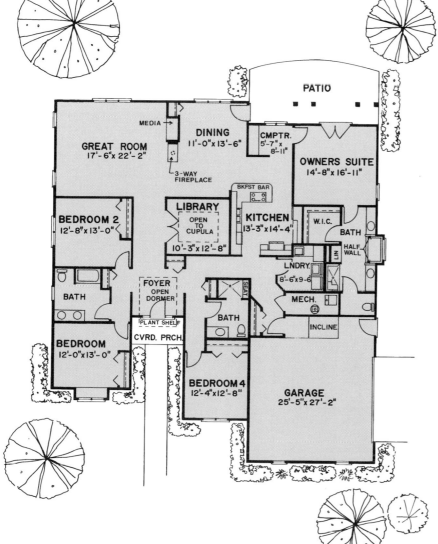

DESIGN HPT01030

Square Footage: 3,018

Price Tier: C2

- Owners suite directly accesses exterior
- Open dormer above entry
- Three-way fireplace separates dining and living rooms
- Laundry may be combined with kitchen or owners bath for future modifications
- Four bedrooms with three full baths
- Library has open cupola for natural light
- Computer or resource center

DESIGN BY
©The Philip Stephen
Companies, Inc.

Width 65'-6"
Depth 67'-0"

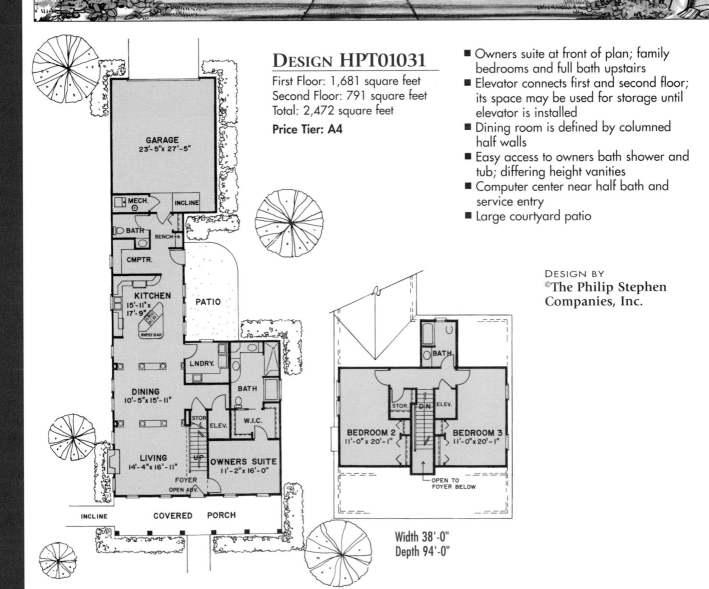

DESIGN HPT01031

First Floor: 1,681 square feet
Second Floor: 791 square feet
Total: 2,472 square feet

Price Tier: A4

- Owners suite at front of plan; family bedrooms and full bath upstairs
- Elevator connects first and second floor; its space may be used for storage until elevator is installed
- Dining room is defined by columned half walls
- Easy access to owners bath shower and tub; differing height vanities
- Computer center near half bath and service entry
- Large courtyard patio

DESIGN BY
©The Philip Stephen
Companies, Inc.

GARAGE
23'-5" x 27'-5"

MECH.

INCLINE

BATH

BENCH

CMPTR.

KITCHEN
15'-11" x 17'-9"

PATIO

BKFST BAR

LNDRY.

BATH

DINING
10'-5" x 15'-11"

STOR

ELEV.

W.I.C.

LIVING
14'-4" x 16'-11"

UP

OWNERS SUITE
11'-2" x 16'-0"

FOYER
OPEN ABV.

INCLINE

COVERED PORCH

BATH

STOR.

DN

ELEV.

BEDROOM 2
11'-0" x 20'-1"

BEDROOM 3
11'-0" x 20'-1"

OPEN TO
FOYER BELOW

Width 38'-0"
Depth 94'-0"

DESIGN HPT01032

Square Footage: 2,746
Optional Bonus Room: 451 square feet

Price Tier: C1

- Two-story study or optional Bedroom 4 with upper windows for natural light
- Bonus room with vaulted ceiling over garage
- Bedroom 3 has walk-in closet
- Owners suite with maneuverable walk-in closet and generous bath with curbless shower and whirlpool
- Kitchen has flexible table space and room for a rolling cart
- Formal living and dining rooms
- Half bath at service entry

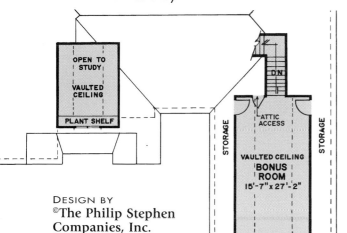

DESIGN BY
©The Philip Stephen
Companies, Inc.

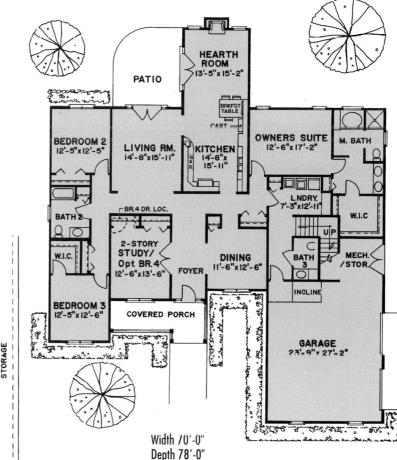

Width 70'-0"
Depth 78'-0"

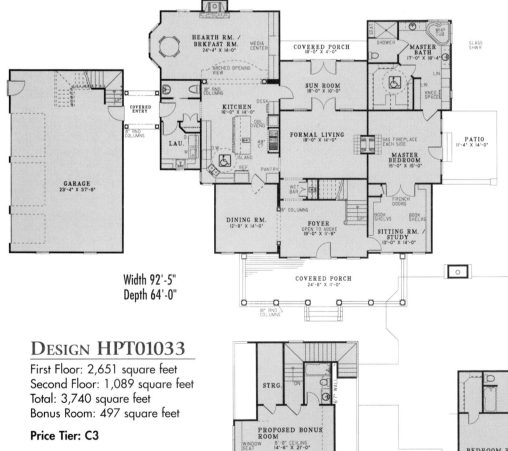

- Two-story foyer separates dining room and sitting room or study
- Formal living room with fireplace and sun room to covered porch
- Hearth room and breakfast room attach to island kitchen
- Three-car garage
- Owners suite with fireplace, private patio and bath
- Two family bedrooms with window seats and private baths on second floor
- Bonus room with window seat and bath

Width 92'-5"
Depth 64'-0"

Design HPT01033

First Floor: 2,651 square feet
Second Floor: 1,089 square feet
Total: 3,740 square feet
Bonus Room: 497 square feet

Price Tier: C3

Design by
©**Michael E. Nelson,**
Nelson Design Group, LLC

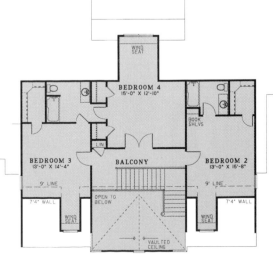

- Study and dining room with French doors to great room
- Computer center off great room
- Screened porch accessed at four points
- Large owners suite with dual walk-in closets and exercise or hobby room
- Two family bedrooms with shared bath on second floor
- Optional media room
- Kitchen has eat-in bar

DESIGN HPT01034

First Floor: 2,473 square feet
Second Floor: 1,233 square feet
Total: 3,706 square feet
Optional Media Room: 155 square feet

Price Tier: C3

DESIGN BY
©Michael E. Nelson,
Nelson Design Group, LLC

3-CAR GARAGE
24'-0" X 36'-4"
GARAGE LOCATION TO BE DETERMINED

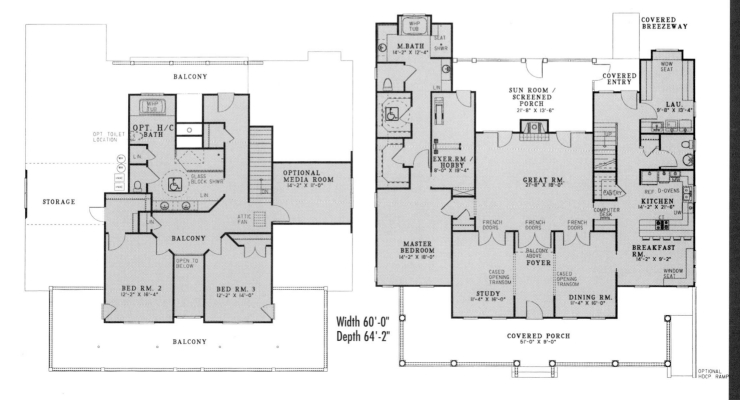

Width 60'-0"
Depth 64'-2"

DESIGN HPT01035

Square Footage: 2,182

Price Tier: A4

- Covered porch and courtyard; exterior door near Bedrooms 2 and 3 for emergency exit
- Computer counter
- Bedroom 3 may be converted to semi-private suite and has built-in desk
- Owners bath with separate tub and shower, compartmented toilet and two different height vanities
- Great room, plus family room/dining room combination
- Breezeway connects garage to main home

DESIGN BY
©The Philip Stephen Companies, Inc.

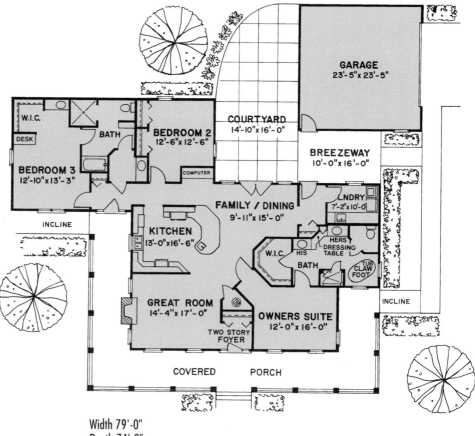

Width 79'-0"
Depth 74'-0"

DECK

OWNERS SUITE
14'-0" x 17'-1"

DINING
9'-10" x 14'-0"

BKFST. BAR
SKYLIGHT

GREAT ROOM
15'-5" x 23'-10"
x 14'-0"

KITCHEN
14'-0" x 15'-2"

LNDRY
7'-0"
x 14'-0"

LNDRY PASS-THRU.

3 SIDED FIREPLACE

W.I.C.

HALF WALL

SEAT SEAT

ELEV.

HALF WALL

M. BATH

W.I.C.

DN

BATH 2

INCLINE

GALLERY

STUDY / BR 3
14'-0" x 17'-1"

OPEN TO ABOVE

FOYER

GUEST / BR 2
13'-7" x 17'-1"

GARAGE
23'-5" x 35'-8"

COVERED   PORCH

DESIGN HPT01036

Main Level: 2,611 square feet
Lower Level: 1,073 square feet
Total: 3,684 square feet

Price Tier: C3

DESIGN BY
©The Philip Stephen Companies, Inc.

Width 91'-0"
Depth 57'-6"

- Elevator connects lower level and main level
- Central gallery is hub for living and sleeping areas
- Exercise room with full bath on lower level may become caregiver's suite
- Recreation room features kitchenette
- Bedroom 3 could become a study
- Skylit breakfast bar
- Maneuverable walk-in closet, accommodating dual-access bath with curbless shower and whirlpool and a laundry pass-through in owners suite

UNFINISHED
16'-0" x 16'-10"

WORKOUT
12'-7" x 14'-11"

RECREATION
21'-1" x 23'-1"

KITCHENETTE

BATH 3

ELEV.

STOR.

UP

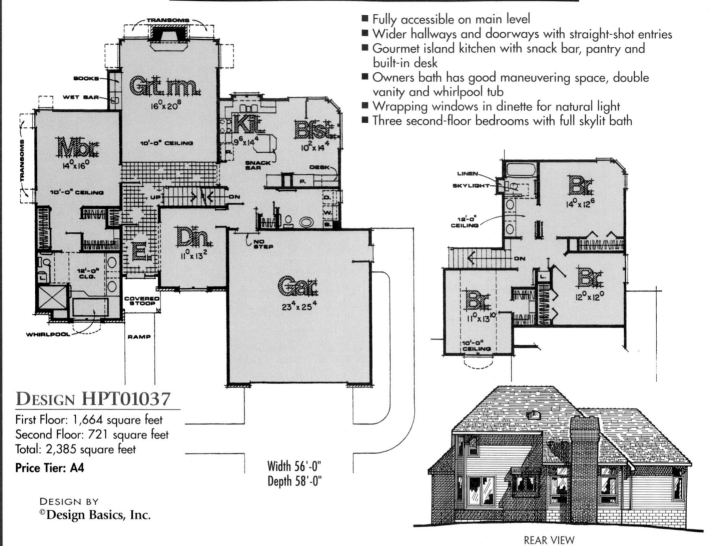

- Fully accessible on main level
- Wider hallways and doorways with straight-shot entries
- Gourmet island kitchen with snack bar, pantry and built-in desk
- Owners bath has good maneuvering space, double vanity and whirlpool tub
- Wrapping windows in dinette for natural light
- Three second-floor bedrooms with full skylit bath

DESIGN HPT01037

First Floor: 1,664 square feet
Second Floor: 721 square feet
Total: 2,385 square feet

Price Tier: A4

Width 56'-0"
Depth 58'-0"

DESIGN BY
©**Design Basics, Inc.**

REAR VIEW

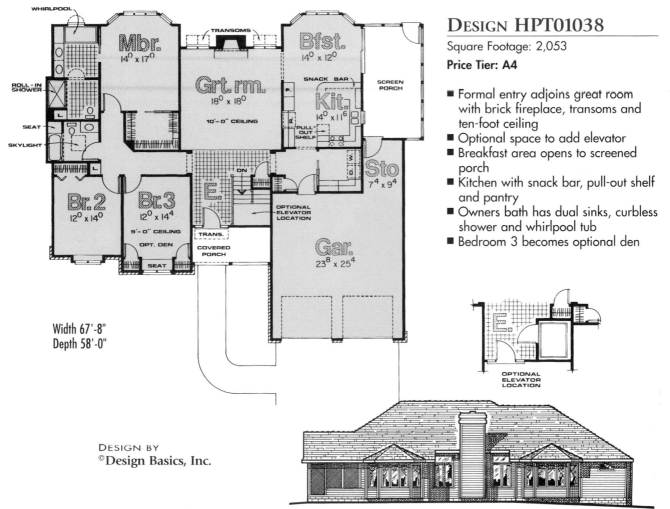

DESIGN HPT01038

Square Footage: 2,053

Price Tier: A4

- Formal entry adjoins great room with brick fireplace, transoms and ten-foot ceiling
- Optional space to add elevator
- Breakfast area opens to screened porch
- Kitchen with snack bar, pull-out shelf and pantry
- Owners bath has dual sinks, curbless shower and whirlpool tub
- Bedroom 3 becomes optional den

Width 67'-8"
Depth 58'-0"

DESIGN BY
©Design Basics, Inc.

REAR VIEW

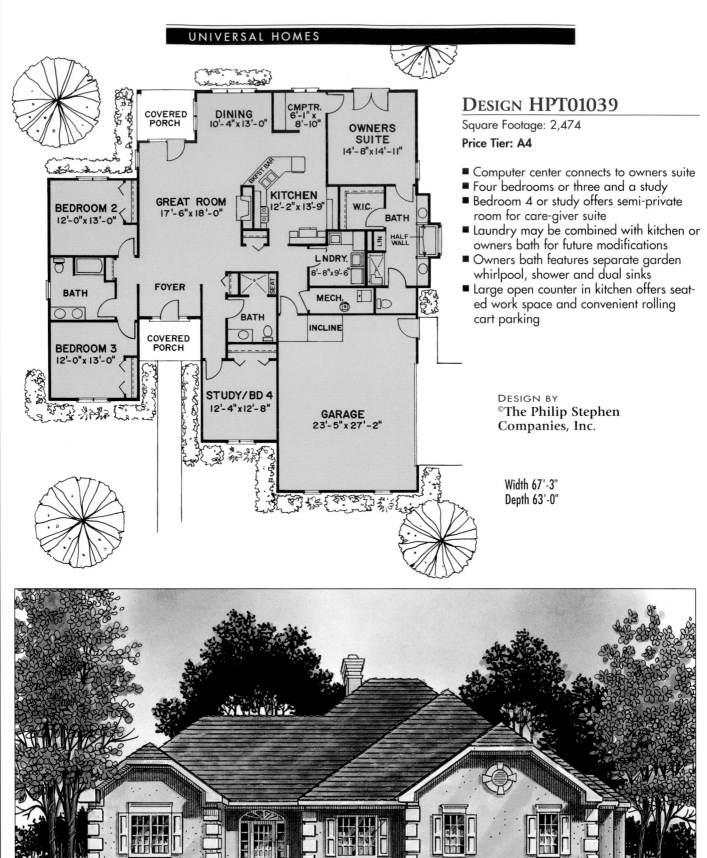

COVERED PORCH

DINING
10'-4"x13'-0"

CMPTR.
6'-1" x
8'-10"

OWNERS SUITE
14'-8"x14'-11"

BEDROOM 2
12'-0"x13'-0"

GREAT ROOM
17'-6"x18'-0"

KITCHEN
12'-2"x13'-9"

BKFST BAR

W.I.C.

BATH

BATH

FOYER

LIN

HALF WALL

LNDRY.
8'-8"x9'-6"

MECH.

BEDROOM 3
12'-0"x13'-0"

COVERED PORCH

BATH

SEAT

INCLINE

STUDY/BD 4
12'-4"x12'-8"

GARAGE
23'-5"x27'-2"

Design HPT01039

Square Footage: 2,474

Price Tier: A4

- Computer center connects to owners suite
- Four bedrooms or three and a study
- Bedroom 4 or study offers semi-private room for care-giver suite
- Laundry may be combined with kitchen or owners bath for future modifications
- Owners bath features separate garden whirlpool, shower and dual sinks
- Large open counter in kitchen offers seated work space and convenient rolling cart parking

Design by
©The Philip Stephen Companies, Inc.

Width 67'-3"
Depth 63'-0"

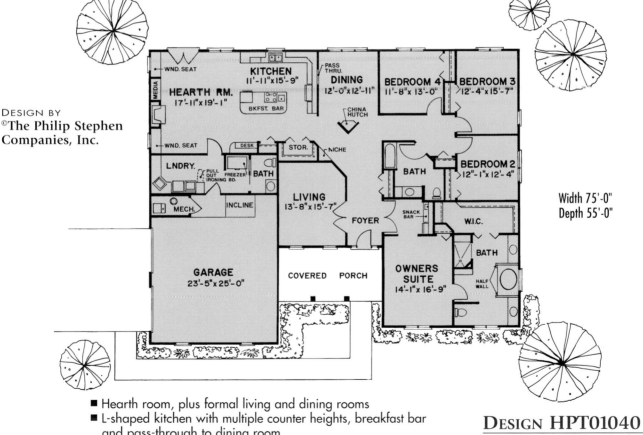

DESIGN BY
©The Philip Stephen
Companies, Inc.

WND. SEAT

MEDIA

KITCHEN
11'-11"x15'-9"

HEARTH RM.
17'-11"x19'-1"

BKFST. BAR

PASS THRU.

DINING
12'-0"x12'-11"

BEDROOM 4
11'-8"x 13'-0"

BEDROOM 3
12'-4"x 15'-7"

CHINA HUTCH

WND. SEAT

DESK

STOR.

NICHE

LNDRY.

PULL OUT IRONING BD.

FREEZER

BATH

LIVING
13'-8"x 15'-7"

BATH

BEDROOM 2
12'-1"x 12'-4"

MECH.

INCLINE

FOYER

SNACK BAR

W.I.C.

GARAGE
23'-5"x 25'-0"

COVERED   PORCH

OWNERS SUITE
14'-1"x 16'-9"

BATH

HALF WALL

Width 75'-0"
Depth 55'-0"

- Hearth room, plus formal living and dining rooms
- L-shaped kitchen with multiple counter heights, breakfast bar and pass-through to dining room
- Second kitchen sink with pull-out sprayer to reach cooktop
- Four bedrooms and two full baths
- Snack bar outside of owners bedroom
- Owners bath has differing height sinks, curbless shower, soaking tub and generous closet
- Laundry with pull-out ironing board, freezer space and half bath

DESIGN HPT01040

Square Footage: 2,971

Price Tier: C1

COPYRIGHT LARRY E. BELK

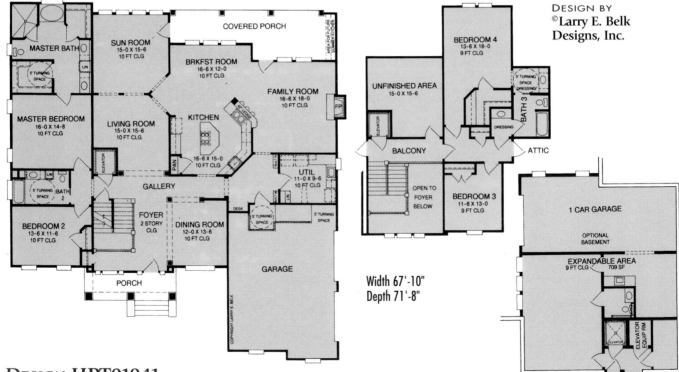

DESIGN BY
©**Larry E. Belk
Designs, Inc.**

Width 67'-10"
Depth 71'-8"

DESIGN HPT01041

First Floor: 2,861 square feet
Second Floor: 783 square feet
Total: 3,644 square feet
Optional Basement: 709 square feet

Price Tier: C3

- Elevator connects first and second floors or optional basement
- Owners suite with walk-in closets and bath with curbless shower
- Roll-under sinks in kitchen and owners bath
- Two family bedrooms with full bath on second floor
- An additional one-car garage and expandable space in option-al basement
- Garage with eight-foot-high door and ramp

DESIGN HPT01042

First Floor: 1,814 square feet
Second Floor: 923 square feet
Total: 2,737 square feet

Price Tier: C1

DESIGN BY
©Alan Mascord
Design Associates, Inc.

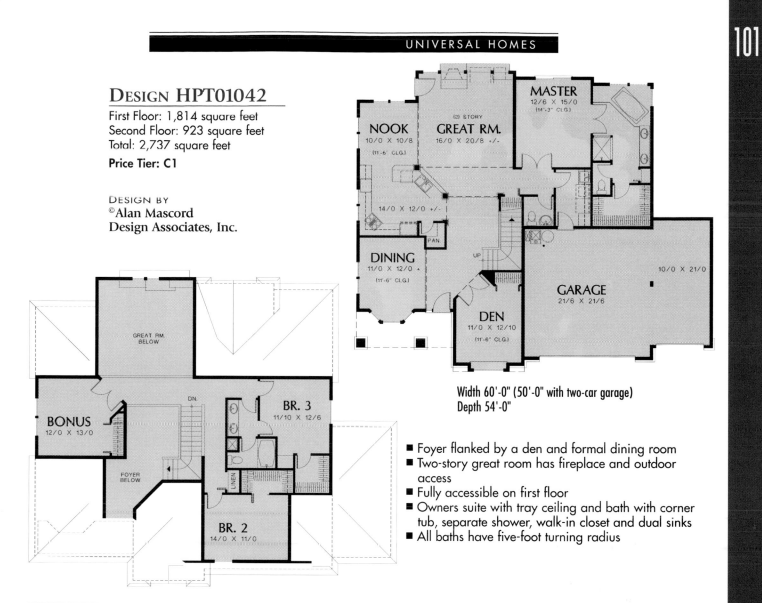

NOOK
10/0 X 10/8
(11'-6" CLG.)

GREAT RM.
16/0 X 20/8 +/-

(2) STORY

MASTER
12/6 X 15/0
(14'-3" CLG.)

14/0 X 12/0 +/-

DINING
11/0 X 12/0 +
(11'-6" CLG.)

PAN.

UP

DEN
11/0 X 12/10
(11'-6" CLG.)

GARAGE
21/6 X 21/6

10/0 X 21/0

GREAT RM.
BELOW

BONUS
12/0 X 13/0

DN.

BR. 3
11/10 X 12/6

FOYER
BELOW

LINEN

BR. 2
14/0 X 11/0

Width 60'-0" (50'-0" with two-car garage)
Depth 54'-0"

- Foyer flanked by a den and formal dining room
- Two-story great room has fireplace and outdoor access
- Fully accessible on first floor
- Owners suite with tray ceiling and bath with corner tub, separate shower, walk-in closet and dual sinks
- All baths have five-foot turning radius

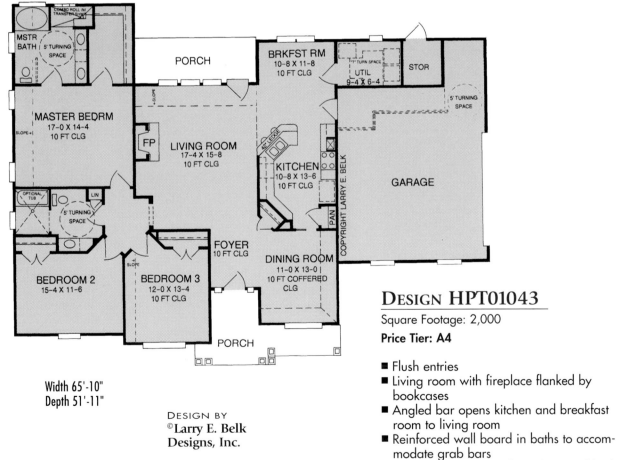

Width 65'-10"
Depth 51'-11"

DESIGN BY
©Larry E. Belk
Designs, Inc.

DESIGN HPT01043

Square Footage: 2,000

Price Tier: A4

- Flush entries
- Living room with fireplace flanked by bookcases
- Angled bar opens kitchen and breakfast room to living room
- Reinforced wall board in baths to accommodate grab bars
- Owners suite with walk-in closet and bath with five-foot turning radius

This home, as shown in the photograph, may differ from the actual blueprints. For more detailed information, please check the floor plans carefully.

Photo by Living Concepts Home Planning

DESIGN BY
©Living Concepts
Home Planning

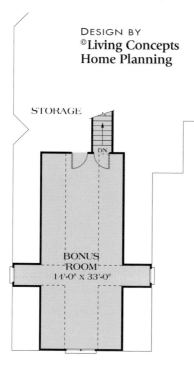

STORAGE

DN

BONUS ROOM
14'-0" x 33'-0"

GATHERING ROOM
10'-0" x 10'-0"

BREAKFAST
10'-0" x 9'-0"

COVERED LANAI

SITTING AREA

GRAND ROOM
14'-4" x 16'-0"

MASTER RETREAT
15'-0" x 19'-0"

KITCHEN
13'-10" x 13'-6"

PANT

W.I.C.

SUITE 2
11'-6" x 14'-8"

W.I.C.

UP

DINING ROOM
11'-2" x 15'-4"

FOYER

MASTER BATH

BATH

PDR.

LOGGIA

OPT. DN

LAUNDRY

SUITE 3
13'-0" x 11'-6"

W.I.C.

Width 61'-0"
Depth 80'-0"

GARAGE
22'-10" x 25'-0"

- Fully accessible on one level with flush entries
- First-floor owners retreat features tray ceiling and open bath with double walk-in closets, separate tub and shower
- Family bedrooms separated by full bath
- Casual gathering room with fireplace open to breakfast nook and kitchen
- Natural light throughout

DESIGN HPT01044

Square Footage: 2,585 (2,621 for basement plan)
Bonus Room: 519 square feet

Price Tier: C1

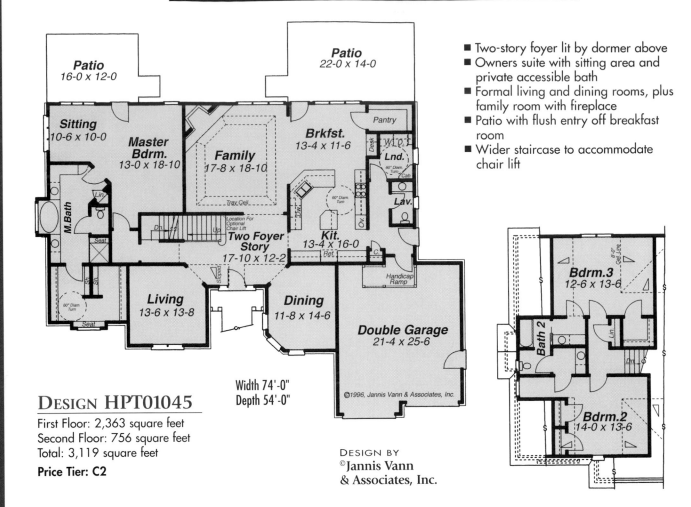

Patio
16-0 x 12-0

Patio
22-0 x 14-0

Sitting
10-6 x 10-0

Master Bdrm.
13-0 x 18-10

Family
17-8 x 18-10

Brkfst.
13-4 x 11-6

Pantry

M. Bath

Lin

Trav. Cell

W.D.

Lnd.

Lav.

Desk

60" Diam. Turn

Location For Optional Chair Lift

60" Diam. Turn

Dn

Up

Two Story Foyer
17-10 x 12-2

Kit.
13-4 x 16-0

Seat

60" Diam Turn

Seat

Living
13-6 x 13-8

Dining
11-8 x 14-6

Handicap Ramp

Double Garage
21-4 x 25-6

Width 74'-0"
Depth 54'-0"

© 1996, Jannis Vann & Associates, Inc.

Bath 2

Bdrm.3
12-6 x 13-6

8'-0" Ceil. Line

Bdrm.2
14-0 x 13-6

- Two-story foyer lit by dormer above
- Owners suite with sitting area and private accessible bath
- Formal living and dining rooms, plus family room with fireplace
- Patio with flush entry off breakfast room
- Wider staircase to accommodate chair lift

DESIGN HPT01045

First Floor: 2,363 square feet
Second Floor: 756 square feet
Total: 3,119 square feet

Price Tier: C2

DESIGN BY
© Jannis Vann
& Associates, Inc.

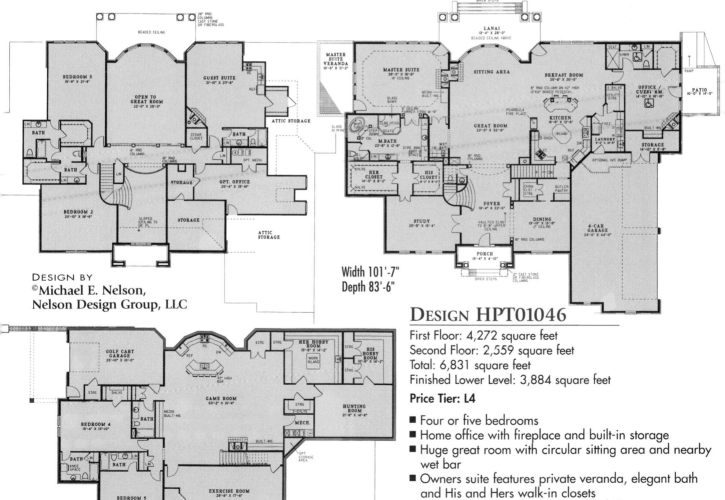

DESIGN BY
©Michael E. Nelson,
Nelson Design Group, LLC

Width 101'-7"
Depth 83'-6"

DESIGN HPT01046

First Floor: 4,272 square feet
Second Floor: 2,559 square feet
Total: 6,831 square feet
Finished Lower Level: 3,884 square feet

Price Tier: L4

- Four or five bedrooms
- Home office with fireplace and built-in storage
- Huge great room with circular sitting area and nearby wet bar
- Owners suite features private veranda, elegant bath and His and Hers walk-in closets
- Study and formal dining room flank foyer
- Butler's pantry connects dining room to island kitchen
- All second-floor bedrooms have walk-in closets
- Guest suite has private bath and fireplace

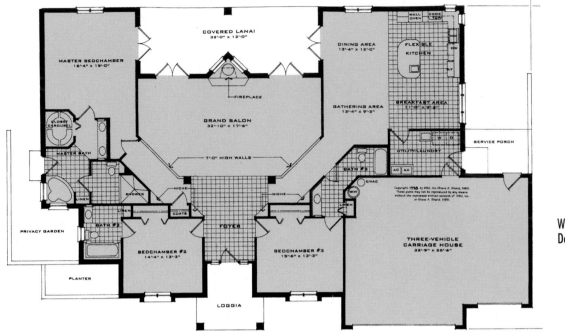

Width 88'-0"
Depth 58'-0"

DESIGN HPT01047

Square Footage: 2,907

Price Tier: C4

DESIGN BY
©**Design Services
Unlimited, Inc.**

- Two flexible, accessible bathrooms
- Central vacuum system
- Owners bath with privacy garden, curbless shower, side-load toilet and whirlpool tub
- Three-car garage with eight-foot-high by eighteen-foot-wide door
- Accessible on one level with no steps
- Closet carousel
- Reinforced ceilings in bedroom and bath for overhead tracks
- Reproducible sepias not available for this plan

Design by
©**Design Services
Unlimited, Inc.**

Width 84'-0"
Depth 69'-0"

- Owners suite with two walk-in closets and bath with curbless shower, whirlpool tub and dual sinks
- Accessible on the first floor with no steps
- Formal parlor with fireplace and built-ins
- Three-car garage with eight-foot-high by eighteen-foot-wide door
- Second-floor billiards room and bedroom with full bath
- Reinforced ceilings in bedroom and bath for overhead tracks
- Central vacuum system
- Reproducible sepias not available for this plan

DESIGN HPT01048

First Floor: 3,462 square feet
Second Floor: 521 square feet
Total: 3,983 square feet

Price Tier: L1

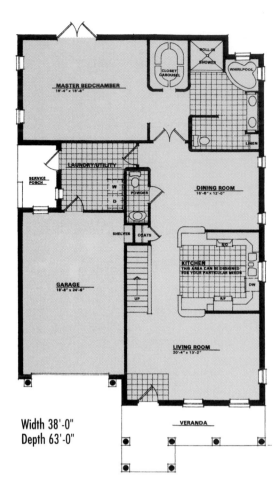

Width 38'-0"
Depth 63'-0"

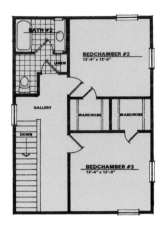

- Accessible on one floor with no steps
- Owners bath with large whirlpool tub, curbless shower and double sinks
- Closet carousel in owners suite walk-in
- All doors at least three-feet wide (including most interior doors)
- Two bedrooms and full bath on second floor
- Reproducible sepias not available for this plan

DESIGN HPT01049

First Floor: 1,507 square feet
Second Floor: 620 square feet
Total: 2,127 square feet

Price Tier: C2

DESIGN BY
©Design Services
Unlimited, Inc.

This home, as shown in the photograph, may differ from the actual blueprints.
For more detailed information, please check the floor plans carefully.

Photo by Kevin Berne

DESIGN HPT01050

Square Footage: 3,187

Price Tier: L1

- Skylights throughout the home
- Two separate garages with ramp in Garage 2
- Owners suite is self-contained with kitchenette, den and bath with curbless shower and knee-space counter
- Back entry designed to access deck for flush access; flush front entry
- Family room with skylights, built-ins and fireplace
- Lifestages Home

DESIGN BY
©Home Planners

Width 77'-8"
Depth 72'-4"

Ordering Home Plans

Before filling out the coupon at right or calling us on our Toll-Free Blueprint Hotline, you may want to learn more about our services and products. Here's some information you will find helpful.

Quick Turnaround

We process and ship every blueprint order from our office within two business days. Because of this quick turnaround, we won't send a formal notice acknowledging receipt of your order.

Our Exchange Policy

Since blueprints are printed in response to your order, we cannot honor requests for refunds. However, we will exchange your entire first order for an equal number of blueprints at a price of $50 for the first set and $10 for each additional set; $70 total exchange fee for 4 sets; $100 total exchange fee for 8 sets . . . *plus* the difference in cost if exchanging for a design in a higher price bracket or *less* the difference in cost if exchanging for a design in lower price bracket. One exchange is allowed within a year of purchase date. **(Sepias and reproducibles are not refundable, returnable or exchangeable.)** All sets from the first order must be returned before the exchange can take place. Please add $18 for postage and handling via Regular Service; $30 via Priority Service; $40 via Express Service. Returns and cancellations are subject to a 20% restocking fee, and shipping and handling charges are not refundable.

About Reverse Blueprints

If you want to build in reverse of the plan as shown, we will include any number of reverse blueprints (mirror image) from a 4- or 8-set package for an additional fee of $50. Although lettering and dimensions will appear backward, reverses will be a useful aid if you decide to flop the plan.

Revising, Modifying and Customizing Plans

The wide variety of designs available in this publication allows you to select ideas and concepts for a home to fit your building site and match your family's needs, wants and budget. Like many homeowners who buy these plans, you and your builder, architect or engineer may want to make changes to them. Some minor changes may be made by your builder, but we recommend that most changes be made by a licensed architect or engineer. As set forth below, we cannot assume any responsibility for blueprints which have been changed, whether by you, your builder or by professionals selected by you or referred to you by us, because such individuals are outside our supervision and control.

Architectural and Engineering Seals

Some cities and states are now requiring that a licensed architect or engineer review and "seal" a blueprint, or officially approve it, prior to construction due to concerns over energy costs, safety and other factors. Prior to application for a building permit or the start of actual construction, we strongly advise that you consult your local building official who can tell you if such a review is required.

About the Designers

The architects and designers whose work appears in this publication are among America's leading residential designers. Each plan was designed to meet the requirements of a nationally recognized model building code in effect at the time and place the plan was drawn. Because national building codes change from time to time, plans may not comply with any such code at the time they are sold to a customer. In addition, building officials may not accept these plans as final construction documents of record as the plans may need to be modified and addi-tional drawings and details added to suit local conditions and requirements. We strongly advise that purchasers consult a licensed architect or engineer and their local building official before starting any construction related to these plans.

Local Building Codes and Zoning Requirements

At the time of creation, our plans are drawn to specifications published by the Building Officials and Code Administrators (BOCA) International, Inc.; the Southern Building Code Congress (SBCCI) International, Inc.; the International Conference of Building Officials; or the Council of American Building Officials (CABO). Our plans are designed to meet or exceed national building standards. Because of the great differences in geography and climate throughout the United States and Canada, each state, county and municipality has its own building codes, zone requirements, ordinances and building regulations. Your plan may need to be modified to comply with local requirements regarding snow loads, energy codes, soil and seismic conditions and a wide range of other matters. In addition, you may need to obtain permits or inspections from local governments before and in the course of construction. Prior to using blueprints ordered from us, we strongly advise that you consult a licensed architect or engineer—and speak with your local building official—before applying for any permit or beginning construction. We authorize the use of our blueprints on the express condition that you strictly comply with all local building codes, zoning requirements and other applicable laws, regulations, ordinances and requirements. **Notice:** Plans for homes to be built in Nevada must be re-drawn by a Nevada-registered professional. Consult your building official for more information on this subject.

Foundation and Exterior Wall Changes

Most of our plans are drawn with either a full or partial basement foundation. Depending on your specific climate or regional building practices, you may wish to change this basement to a slab or crawlspace. Most professional contractors and builders can easily adapt your plans to alternate foundation types. Likewise, most can easily change 2x4 wall construction to 2x6, or vice versa.

Disclaimer

We and the designers we work with have put substantial care and effort into the creation of our blueprints. However, because we cannot provide on-site consultation, supervision and control over actual construction, and because of the great variance in local building requirements, building practices and soil, seismic, weather and other conditions, WE CANNOT MAKE ANY WARRANTY, EXPRESS OR IMPLIED, WITH RESPECT TO THE CONTENT OR USE OF OUR BLUE-PRINTS, INCLUDING BUT NOT LIMITED TO ANY WARRANTY OF MER-CHANTABILITY OR OF FITNESS FOR A PARTICULAR PURPOSE.

Terms and Conditions

These designs are protected under the terms of United States Copyright Law and may not be copied or reproduced in any way, by any means, unless you have purchased Sepias or Reproducibles which clearly indicate your right to copy or reproduce. We authorize the use of your chosen design as an aid in the construction of one single family home only. You may not use this design to build a second or multiple dwellings without purchasing another blueprint or blueprints or paying additional design fees.

How Many Blueprints Do You Need?

A single set of blueprints is sufficient to study a home in greater detail. However, if you are planning to obtain cost estimates from a contractor or subcontractors—or if you are planning to build immediately—you will need more sets. Because additional sets are cheaper when ordered in quantity with the original order, make sure you order enough blueprints to satisfy all requirements. The following check-list will help you determine how many you need:

_____ Owner

_____ Builder (generally requires at least three sets; one as a legal document, one to use during inspections, and at least one to give to subcontractors)

_____ Local Building Department (often requires two sets)

_____ Mortgage Lender (usually one set for a conventional loan; three sets for FHA or VA loans)

_____ TOTAL NUMBER OF SETS

Canadian Customers
Order Toll-Free 877-223-6389

For faster service, Canadian customers may now call in orders directly to our Canadian supplier of plans and charge the purchase to a credit card. Or, you may complete the order form at right, adding the current exchange rate to all prices, and mail in Canadian funds to:

Home Planners Canada
c/o Select Home Designs
301-611 Alexander Street
Vancouver, Canada V6A 1E1

OR: Copy the Order Form and send it via our Canadian FAX line: 1-800-224-6699.

Price Schedule

Blueprint Price Schedule
(Prices guaranteed through December 31, 2000)

Tiers	1-set Study Package	4-set Building Package	8-set Building Package	1-set Reproducible Sepias
A1	$400	$440	$500	$600
A2	$440	$480	$540	$660
A3	$480	$520	$580	$720
A4	$520	$560	$620	$780
C1	$560	$600	$660	$840
C2	$600	$640	$700	$900
C3	$650	$690	$750	$950
C4	$700	$740	$800	$1000
L1	$750	$790	$850	$1050
L2	$800	$840	$900	$1100
L3	$900	$940	$1000	$1200
L4	$1000	$1040	$1100	$1300

Options for plans in Tiers A1-L4
Additional Identical Blueprints in same order for "A1-L4"
  price plans ....$50 per set
Reverse Blueprints (mirror image) with 4- or 8-set order for
  "A1-L4" price plans ....$50 fee per order

Refer to the Price Schedule above to find the price for the Universal home plans you wish to purchase. Note the Price Tier of the plan and match it to the prices above for the cost of one, four, or eight sets of blueprints or the cost of a reproducible sepia. Additional prices are shown for identical and reverse blueprints sets.

To order: Fill in and send the order form at right, or call toll free 1-800-521-6797 or 520-297-8200. FAX: 1-800-224-6699 or 520-544-3086.

Toll Free 1-800-521-6797

Regular Office Hours:
8:00 a.m. to 8:00 p.m. Eastern Time, Monday through Friday Our staff will gladly answer any questions during regular office hours. Our answering service can place orders after hours or on weekends.

If we receive your order by 4:00 p.m. Eastern Time, Monday through Friday, we'll process it and ship within two business days. When ordering by phone, please have your credit card ready. We'll also ask you for the Order Form Key Number at the bottom of the coupon.
By FAX: Copy the Order Form on this page and send it on our
  FAX line:
    1-800-224-6699 or 1-520-544-3086.

 ORDER TOLL FREE!
For information about any of our services or to order call 1-800-521-6797 or 520-297-8200. PLUS Browse our website: www.homeplanners.com

For Customer Service, call toll free 1-888-690-1116.

BLUEPRINTS ARE NOT REFUNDABLE

ORDER FORM

 HOME PLANNERS, LLC
Wholly owned by Hanley-Wood, LLC
3275 WEST INA ROAD, SUITE 110
TUCSON, ARIZONA 85741

THE BASIC BLUEPRINT PACKAGE
Rush me the following (please refer to the Price Schedule in this section):

_____ Set(s) of blueprints for plan number(s)_____. $_____
_____ Set(s) of sepias for plan number(s)_____. $_____
_____ Additional identical blueprints (standard or reverse)
        in same order @ $50 per set. $_____
_____ Reverse blueprints @ $50 fee per order. $_____

POSTAGE AND HANDLING	1–3 sets	4+ sets
Signature is required for all deliveries. **DELIVERY** No CODs (Requires street address—No P.O. Boxes)		
•Regular Service (Allow 7–10 business days delivery)	❏ $15.00	❏ $18.00
•Priority (Allow 4–5 business days delivery)	❏ $20.00	❏ $30.00
•Express (Allow 3 business days delivery)	❏ $30.00	❏ $40.00
CERTIFIED MAIL (Requires signature) If no street address available. (Allow 7–10 days delivery)	❏ $20.00	❏ $30.00
OVERSEAS DELIVERY Note: All delivery times are from date Blueprint Package is shipped.	fax, phone or mail for quote	

POSTAGE (From box above) $_____
SUBTOTAL $_____
SALES TAX (AZ, MI & WA residents, please add
            appropriate state and local sales tax.) $_____
TOTAL (Subtotal and tax) $_____

YOUR ADDRESS (please print)

Name _____

Street _____

City_____State_____Zip _____

Daytime telephone number (_____) _____

FOR CREDIT CARD ORDERS ONLY
Please fill in the information below:

Credit card number _____

Exp. Date: Month/Year _____

Check one ❏ Visa ❏ MasterCard ❏ Discover Card ❏ American Express

Signature _____

Please check appropriate box: ❏ Licensed Builder-Contractor
                                ❏ Homeowner

 **ORDER TOLL FREE!**
1-800-521-6797 or 520-297-8200

Order Form Key

HPT01

Helpful Books & Software

Home Planners wants your building experience to be as pleasant and trouble-free as possible. That's why we've expanded our library of Do-It-Yourself titles to help you along. In addition to our beautiful plans books, we've added books to guide you through specific projects as well as the construction process. In fact, these are titles that will be as useful after your dream home is built as they are right now.

ONE-STORY
1 448 designs for all lifestyles. 860 to 5,400 square feet. 384 pages $9.95

TWO-STORY
2 460 designs for one-and-a-half and two stories. 1,245 to 7,275 square feet. 384 pages $9.95

VACATION
3 345 designs for recreation, retirement and leisure. 312 pages $8.95

MULTI-LEVEL
4 214 designs for split-levels, bi-levels, multi-levels and walkouts. 224 pages $8.95

COUNTRY
5 200 country designs from classic to contemporary by 7 winning designers. 224 pages $8.95

MOVE-UP
6 200 stylish designs for today's growing families from 9 hot designers. 224 pages $8.95

NARROW-LOT
7 200 unique homes less than 60-feet wide from 7 designers. Up to 3,000 square feet. 224 pages $8.95

SMALL HOUSE
8 200 beautiful designs chosen for versatility and affordability. 224 pages $8.95

BUDGET-SMART
9 200 efficient plans from 7 top designers, that you can really afford to build! 224 pages $8.95

EXPANDABLES
10 200 flexible plans that expand with your needs from 7 top designers. 240 pages $8.95

ENCYCLOPEDIA
11 500 exceptional plans for all styles and budgets—the best book of its kind! 352 pages $9.95

AFFORDABLE
12 Completely revised and updated, featuring 300 designs for modest budgets. 256 pages $9.95

ENCYCLOPEDIA 2
13 500 completely new plans. Spacious and stylish designs for every budget and taste. 352 pages $9.95

VICTORIAN
14 160 striking Victorian and Farmhouse designs from three leading designers. 192 pages $12.95

ESTATE
15 Dream big! Twenty-one designers showcase their biggest and best plans. 208 pages. $15.95

LUXURY
16 154 fine luxury plans—loaded with luscious amenities! 192 pages $14.95

COTTAGES
17 25 fresh new designs that are as warm as a tropical breeze. A blend of the best aspects of many coastal styles. 64 pages. $19.95

BEST SELLERS
18 Our 50th Anniversary book with 200 of our very best designs in full color! 224 pages $12.95

SPECIAL COLLECTION
19 70 romantic house plans that capture the classic tradition of home design. 160 pages $17.95

COUNTRY HOUSES
20 208 unique home plans that combine traditional style and modern livability. 224 pages $9.95

CLASSIC
21 Timeless, elegant designs that always feel like home. Gorgeous plans that are as flexible and up-to-date as their occupants. 240 pages. $9.95

CONTEMPORARY
22 The most complete and imaginative collection of contemporary designs available anywhere. 240 pages. $9.95

EASY-LIVING
23 200 efficient and sophisticated plans that are small in size, but big on livability. 224 pages $8.95

SOUTHERN
24 207 homes rich in Southern styling and comfort. 240 pages $8.95

SUNBELT
25 215 designs that capture the spirit of the Southwest. 208 pages $10.95

WESTERN
26 215 designs that capture the spirit and diversity of the Western lifestyle. 208 pages $9.95

ENERGY GUIDE
27 The most comprehensive energy efficiency and conservation guide available. 280 pages $35.00

Design Software

BOOK & CD-ROM
28 Both the Home Planners Gold book and matching Windows™ CD-ROM with 3D floorplans. $24.95

3D DESIGN SUITE
29 Home design made easy! View designs in 3D, take a virtual reality tour, add decorating details and more. $59.95

Outdoor Projects

OUTDOOR
30 42 unique outdoor projects. Gazebos, strombellas, bridges, sheds, playsets and more! 96 pages $7.95

GARAGES & MORE
31 101 multi-use garages and outdoor structures to enhance any home. 96 pages $7.95

DECKS
32 25 outstanding single-, double- and multi-level decks you can build. 112 pages $7.95

Landscape Designs

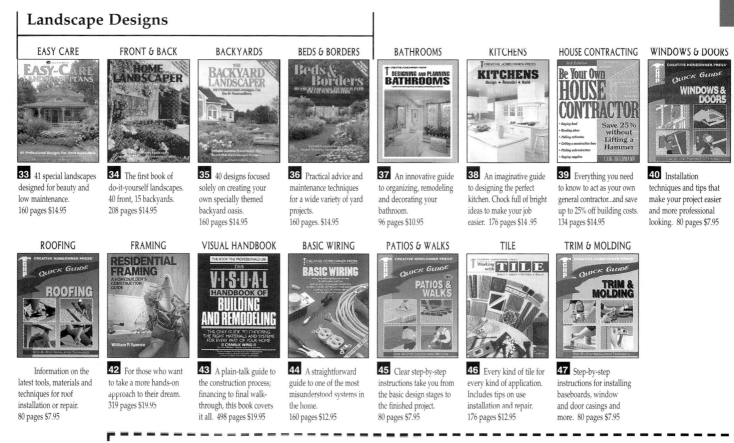

EASY CARE	FRONT & BACK	BACKYARDS	BEDS & BORDERS	BATHROOMS	KITCHENS	HOUSE CONTRACTING	WINDOWS & DOORS

33 41 special landscapes designed for beauty and low maintenance. 160 pages $14.95

34 The first book of do-it-yourself landscapes. 40 front, 15 backyards. 208 pages $14.95

35 40 designs focused solely on creating your own specially themed backyard oasis. 160 pages $14.95

36 Practical advice and maintenance techniques for a wide variety of yard projects. 160 pages. $14.95

37 An innovative guide to organizing, remodeling and decorating your bathroom. 96 pages $10.95

38 An imaginative guide to designing the perfect kitchen. Chock full of bright ideas to make your job easier. 176 pages $14 .95

39 Everything you need to know to act as your own general contractor...and save up to 25% off building costs. 134 pages $14.95

40 Installation techniques and tips that make your project easier and more professional looking. 80 pages $7.95

ROOFING	FRAMING	VISUAL HANDBOOK	BASIC WIRING	PATIOS & WALKS	TILE	TRIM & MOLDING

Information on the latest tools, materials and techniques for roof installation or repair. 80 pages $7.95

42 For those who want to take a more hands-on approach to their dream. 319 pages $19.95

43 A plain-talk guide to the construction process; financing to final walk-through, this book covers it all. 498 pages $19.95

44 A straightforward guide to one of the most misunderstood systems in the home. 160 pages $12.95

45 Clear step-by-step instructions take you from the basic design stages to the finished project. 80 pages $7.95

46 Every kind of tile for every kind of application. Includes tips on use installation and repair. 176 pages $12.95

47 Step-by-step instructions for installing baseboards, window and door casings and more. 80 pages $7.95

Additional Books Order Form

To order your books, just check the box of the book numbered below and complete the coupon. We will process your order and ship it from our office within 48 hours. Send coupon and check (in U.S. funds).

YES! Please send me the books I've indicated:

☐ 1:VO	$9.95	☐ 25:SW	$10.95
☐ 2:VT	$9.95	☐ 26:WH	$9.95
☐ 3:VH	$8.95	☐ 27:RES	$35.00
☐ 4:VS	$8.95	☐ 28:HPGC	$24.95
☐ 5:FH	$8.95	☐ 29:PLANSUITE	$59.95
☐ 6:MU	$8.95	☐ 30:YG	$7.95
☐ 7:NL	$8.95	☐ 31:GG	$7.95
☐ 8:SM	$8.95	☐ 32:DP	$7.95
☐ 9:BS	$8.95	☐ 33:ECL	$14.95
☐ 10:EX	$8.95	☐ 34:HL	$14.95
☐ 11:EN	$9.95	☐ 35:BYL	$14.95
☐ 12:AF	$9.95	☐ 36:BB	$14.95
☐ 13:E2	$9.95	☐ 37:CDB	$10.95
☐ 14:VDH	$12.95	☐ 38:CKI	$14.95
☐ 15:EDH	$15.95	☐ 39:SBC	$14.95
☐ 16:LD2	$14.95	☐ 40:CGD	$7.95
☐ 17:CTG	$19.95	☐ 41:CGR	$7.95
☐ 18:HPG	$12.95	☐ 42:SRF	$19.95
☐ 19:WEP	$17.95	☐ 43:RVH	$19.95
☐ 20:CN	$9.95	☐ 44:CBW	$12.95
☐ 21:CS	$9.95	☐ 45:CGW	$7.95
☐ 22:CM	$9.95	☐ 46:CWT	$12.95
☐ 23:EL	$8.95	☐ 47:CMP	$12.95
☐ 24:SH	$8.95	☐ 48:CGT	$7.95

Canadian Customers
Order Toll Free 1-877-223-6389

Additional Books Subtotal $_____
ADD Postage and Handling $__4.00__
Sales Tax: (AZ, MI, & WA residents, please add appropriate state and local sales tax.) $_____
YOUR TOTAL (Subtotal, Postage/Handling, Tax) $_____

YOUR ADDRESS (Please print)

Name _____

Street _____

City _____ State_____ Zip _____

Phone (_____) _____ — _____

YOUR PAYMENT
Check one: ☐ Check ☐ Visa ☐ MasterCard ☐ Discover Card
☐ American Express
Required credit card information:

Credit Card Number_____

Expiration Date (Month/Year)_____ / _____

Signature Required _____

Home Planners, LLC
Wholly owned by Hanley-Wood, LLC
3275 W Ina Road, Suite 110, Dept. BK, Tucson, AZ 85741

HPT01

Active Living Devices

Activeaid, Inc.
P.O. Box 359
Redwood Falls, MN 56283
800-533-5330
E-mail:
activeaid@activeaid.com
www.activeaid.com

**Bruno Independent
Living Aids, Inc.**
1780 Executive Drive
Oconomowoc, WI 53066
414-567-4990
800-882-8183
FAX: 414-953-5501
E-mail: sgibbs@bruno.com
www.bruno.com

**Jackson Medical
Equipment**
982 Thomas Ave.
St. Paul, MN 55104
651-645-6221

The Life Place
125 W. Market
Mall of America
Bloomington, MN 55425
651-702-0397

Medically Yours
3839 Merle Hay Rd.
Number 170
Des Moines, IA 50310
515-270-0725
FAX: 515-270-0166
E-mail: medyours@aol.com

Owl Home Medical
312 Saint Johns Way
Lewiston, ID 83501
208-743-7766

White and White
3228 W. Carleton Rd.
Hillsdale, MI 49242
517-437-7090
800-258-7816
FAX: 517-437-2260

Services and Resources

Accessibility By Design
2240 E. Central Ave.
Miamisburg, OH 45342
937-866-5115
800-860-3725
FAX: 937-866-6770
E-mail: accessdsgn@
aol.com
members.aol.com/
accessdsgn/page1.html

**Access Information
Bulletins**
Paralyzed Veterans of
America
801 18th Street, NW
Washington, DC 20006
202-872-1300

Access Remodeling
P.O. Box 60027
Potomac, MD 20859
301-983-0131

Adaptive Environments
374 Congress Street
Suite 301
Boston, MA 02210
617-695-1225
FAX: 617-482-8099

**Adaptive
Environments Lab**
State University of New
York at Buffalo
School of Architecture
and Planning
Buffalo, NY 14214
716-645-2000

Ageless Design
12633 159th Court North
Jupiter, FL 33478
561-745-0210
FAX: 561-744-9572
E-mail: agelessd@aol.com
www.agelessdesign.com

**American Association
of Retired Persons**
601 E Street, NW
Washington, DC 20049
202-434-2277

**American Foundation
for the Blind**
11 Pen Plaza
Suite 300
New York, NY 10001
212-502-7600

**American OT
Association, Inc.**
4720 Montgomery Lane
P.O. Box 31220
Bethesda, MD 20824
301-652-2682

**Builders Hardware
Manufacturers
Association**
355 Lexington Ave.
17th Floor
New York, NY 10017
212-297-2122
800-850-8394 Publication
Orders Only
FAX: 212-370-9047
E-mail:
assocmgmt@aol.com
www.buildershardware.
com

**The Center for
Universal Design**
Box 8613
North Carolina State
University
Raleigh, NC 27695
919-515-3082

**CAH Selected
Reading List**
Center for
Universal Design
North Carolina State
University
Box 8613
Raleigh, NC 27695
919-515-3082

**Home Automation
Association**
1444 I Street, N.W.
Suite 700
Washington, DC 20005
202-712-9050
FAX: 202-216-9646
E-mail:
haa@bostromdc.com
www.homeautomation.
org

**International Cast
Polymer Association**
8201 Greensboro Dr.
Suite 300
McLean, VA 22102
703-610-9034
800-414-4272
FAX: 703-610-9005
E-mail: icpa@icpa-hq.com
www.icpa-hq.com

International Mortgage
Owings Mill, MD 21117
410-581-7806
FAX: 410-581-1273

Kephart Architects
770 Sherman Street
Denver, CO 80203
303-832-4474
FAX: 303-832-4476

Life@Home, Inc.
4701 Trousdale Drive
Suite 114
Nashville, TN 37220
800-653-1923
E-mail:
info@lifehome.com
www.lifehome.com

**Low Vision
Information**
The Lighthouse, Inc.
111 East 59th Street
New York, NY 10022
800-334-5497

**Maple Flooring
Manufacturers
Association**
60 Revere Dr.
Suite 500
Northbrook, IL 60062
847-480-9138
FAX: 847-480-9282
E-mail: mfma@
maplefloor.org
www.maplefloor.org

**National Association of
Floor Covering
Distributors**
401 N. Michigan Ave.
Chicago, IL 60611
312-321-6836
FAX: 312-245-1085
E-mail:
mgregory@nafcd.org
www.nafcd.org

**National Council on
Independent Living**
2111 Wilson Blvd.
Suite 405
Arlington, VA 22201
703-525-3406

**The National Council
on Senior Housing**
National Association of
Home Builders
1201 15th Street, NW
Washington, DC 20005
800-368-5242

**National Eldercare
Institute**
Andros Gerontology
Center
University of Southern
California
University Park MC-0191
Los Angeles, CA 90089
213-740-1364

**National Kitchen &
Bath Association
(NKBA)**
687 Willow Grove Street
Hackettstown, NJ 07840
800-THE-NKBA

**Northeast Window and
Door Association**
191 Clarksville Rd.
Princeton Junction, NJ
08550
609-799-4900
FAX: 609-799-7032
E-mail: info@nwda.net
www.nwda.net

Mary Jo Peterson, Inc.
3 Sunset Cove Road
Brookfield, CT 06804
203-775-4763
FAX: 203-740-2333

**The Philip Stephen
Companies, Inc.**
2845 Hamline Avenue
North
Suite 222
Roseville, MN 55113
651-604-0937

Manufacturers & Suppliers Index

Applicances Intl.
Appliances
2807 Antigua Dr.
Burbank, CA 91504
Phone: 888-423-6349
Toll-free: 888-423-6349
Fax: 800-953-9847
Internet: www.appliancesint.com
E-mail: applianceint@1stnctusa.com

AquaGlass
Plumbing, Faucets & Fixtures
P.O. Box 412
Industral Park
Adamsville, TN 38310
Phone: 901-632-0911
Fax: 901-632-1557
Internet: www.AquaGlass.com

Aqua Plunge
Aqua Plunge Div.
Structural Systems
6101 49th St. S.
Muscatine, IA 52761
Phone: 319-263-6642
Toll-free: 800-553-9664
Fax: 319-263-8358

AquaHealth Systems, Inc.
Plumbing, Faucets & Fixtures
2300 S. Clinton Ave.
Unit F
S. Plainfield, NJ 07080
Phone: 908-756-1600
Toll-free: 800-225-7873
Fax: 908-756-1102
Internet: www.epur.com
E-mail: everpure@aol.com

Architectural Landscape Lighting
Landscaping & Outdoor Products
2930 S. Fairview St.
Santa Ana, CA 92704
Toll-free: 800-854-8277
Fax: 714-668-1107
E-mail: alllighting@earthlink.com

Architectural Products by Outwater
Cabinetry; Hardware; Landscaping & Outdoor Products; Specialty Products; Walls, Finishes & Insulation
22 Passaic St.
P.O. Box 347
Wood-Ridge, NJ 07075
Phone: 973-365-2002
Toll-free: 800-835-4400
Fax: 800-835-4403
Internet: www.outwater.com
E-mail: archpro@outwater.com

Ardee Lighting
Electrical & Lighting; Landscaping & Outdoor Products
P.O. Box 1769
Shelby, NC 28151
Phone: 704-482-2811
Toll-free: 800-275-1544

Areslux
Plumbing, Faucets & Fixtures
8229 N.W. 66 St.
Miami, FL 33166
Phone: 305-592-6448
Toll-free: 800-523-1564
Fax: 305-477-5155

Argee Corp.
Landscaping & Outdoor Products
9550 Pathway St.
Santee, CA 92071-4169
Phone: 619-449-5050
Fax: 619-449-8392

Aristokraft
Cabinetry
P.O. Box 420
1 Aristokraft Sq.
Jasper, IN 47547-0420
Phone: 812-482-2527
Fax: 812-482-1763
Internet: www.aristokraft.com

Around The Corner
Walls, Finishes & Insulation
W. 1508 Marsh Rd.
Palmyra, WI 53156
Phone: 414-495-3107
Toll-free: 800-556-7878
Fax: 800-445-3780

Arrow Lock Mfg. Co.
Hardware
103-00 Foster Ave.
Brooklyn, NY 11236
Phone: 718-257-4700
Toll-free: 800-233-0478
Fax: 718-927-1753
Internet: www.arrowlock.com

Artistic Enclosures
Structural Systems
5 Willow St. Industrial Pk.
Fleetwood, PA 19522
Phone: 610-944-8585
Toll-free: 800-944-8599
Fax: 610-944-8120
Internet: www.artisticenclosures.com
E-mail: info@artisticenclosures.com

A-Solution
Windows & Glass
1332 Lobo Pl. N.E.
Albuquerque, NM 87106
Phone: 505-256-0115
Fax: 505-256-3756
Internet: www.windowease.com
E-mail: info@windowease.com

Astracast
Countertops; Plumbing, Faucets & Fixtures
2761 Golfview Dr.
Naperville, IL 60563
Phone: 630-983-4200
Toll-free: 800-276-7726
Fax: 630-983-4662

Auton Motorized Systems
Cabinetry; Specialty Products
P.O. Box 801960
Valencia, CA 91380-1960
Phone: 661-257-9282
Fax: 661-295-5638
Internet: www.auton.com
E-mail: auton@auton.com

AVSI Automated Voice Systems
(MASTERVOICE)
Electrical & Lighting
17059 El Cajon Ave.
Yorba Linda, CA 92886
Phone: 714-524-4488
Fax: 714-996-1127
Internet: www.mastervoice.com
E-mail: gus@hlc.com

B

Barclay Products
Plumbing, Faucets & Fixtures; Specialty Products
4000 Porett Dr.
Gurnee, IL 60031
Phone: 847-244-1234
Toll-free: 800-446-9700
Fax: 847-244-1259

Bask Technologies
HVAC
2867 W. Chestnut Expwy.
Springfield, MO 65802
Phone: 417-522-6128
Toll-free: 888-432-8932
Fax: 417-831-4067
Internet: www.bask.net
E-mail: mfries@bask.net

Bates & Bates
Plumbing, Faucets & Fixtures
3699 Industry Ave.
Lakewood, CA 90712
Phone: 562-595-8824
Toll-free: 800-726-7680
Fax: 562-988-0764
Internet: www.batesinks.com
E-mail: sales@batesinks.com

Bath Ease
Plumbing, Faucets & Fixtures
3815 Darston St.
Palm Harbor, FL 34685-3119
Phone: 727-786-2604
Toll-free: 888-747-7845
Fax: 727-786-2604
E-mail: bathease@aol.com

Bath-Tec Whirlpool Bath
Builder Sales
Plumbing, Faucets & Fixtures
PO Box 1118
Ennis, TX 75120
Phone: 972-646-5279
Toll-free: 800-526-3301
Fax: 972-646-5688
Internet: www.bathtec.com
E-mail: sales@bathtec.com

Beacon/Morris
HVAC
260 N. Elm St.
Westfield, MA 01085
Phone: 413-562-5423
Fax: 413-562-8437

Benchmark Door Systems
(A Div. of General Products Co.)
Doors—Exterior
P.O. Box 7387
Fredericksburg, VA 22404-7387
Phone: 540-898-5700
Toll-free: 800-755-DOOR
Fax: 540-898-5802
Internet: www.benchmark.hw.net

Bennett Industries
Doors—Exterior; Doors—Interior; Structural Systems; Windows & Glass
1530 Palisade Ave.
Fort Lee, NJ 07024
Phone: 201-947-5340
Fax: 201-947-3908

Birchcraft Kitchens
Cabinetry
1612 Thorn St.
Reading, PA 19601
Phone: 610-375-4391
Fax: 610-375-2762

Bird-X
Electrical & Lighting
300 N. Elizabeth St.
Chicago, IL 60607
Phone: 312-226-2473
Fax: 312-226-2480
Internet: www.bird-x.com
E-mail: birdxinc@aol.com

Boa-Franc
Flooring
1255 98th St.
St. Georges, Beauce, PQ
G5Y 8J5 Canada
Phone: 418-227-1181
Fax: 418-227-1188
Internet: www.boa-franc.com
E-mail: mirage@boa-franc.com

Boen Hardwood Flooring
Flooring
350 Hollie Dr.
Bowles Industrial Park
Martinsville, VA 24112
Phone: 540-638-3700
Fax: 540-638-3066
Internet: www.boen.com
E-mail: sales@boen.com

Boiardi Products Corp.
Flooring
453 Main St.
Little Falls, NJ 07424
Phone: 973-256-1100
Toll-free: 800-352-8668
Fax: 973-256-5744

Bomanite Corp.
Landscaping & Outdoor Products
P.O. Box 599
Madera, CA 93639-0599
Phone: 559-673-2411
Fax: 559-673-8246
Internet: www.bomanite.com
E-mail: bomanite@bomanite.com

Brass Accents by Urfic
Hardware
1000 S. Broadway
P.O. Box 110
Salem, OH 44460
Phone: 330-332-9500
Fax: 330-337-8775
E-mail: salem-urfic@att.net

Braun Elevator Co.
Electrical & Lighting; Specialty Products
2829 Royal Ave.
Madison, WI 53713-1541
Phone: 608-221-4400

Brite Millwork
Landscaping & Outdoor Products
641 Hardwick Rd.
Bolton, ON L7E 5R2 Canada
Phone: 905-857-6021
Toll-free: 800-265-6021
Fax: 905-857-3211
Internet: www.britemillwork.com

Broan-NuTone
Electrical & Lighting; HVAC; Specialty Products
926 W. State St.
P.O. Box 140
Hartford, WI 53027-1098
Phone: 414-673-4340
Toll-free: 800-445-6057
Fax: 800-356-5862

Bruce Hardwood Floors
An Armstrong Company
Flooring
16803 Dallas Pkwy.
Addison, TX 75001
Phone: 214-887-2100
Toll-free: 800-722-4647
Fax: 214-887-2234
Internet: www.brucehardwoodfloors.com

Bruce Laminate Floors
An Armstrong Company
Flooring
16803 Dallas Pkwy.
Addison, TX 75001
Phone: 214-887-2100
Toll-free: 800-722-4647
Fax: 214-887-2234
Internet: www.brucelaminatefloors.com

Bruno Independent Living Aids, Inc.
Specialty Products
1780 Executive Dr.
Oconomowoc, WI 53066
Phone: 414-567-4990
Toll-free: 800-882-8183
Fax: 414-953-5501
Internet: www.bruno.com
E-mail: sgibbs@bruno.com

Burgess Intl. Bath Fixtures
Plumbing, Faucets & Fixtures
6810-B Metroplex
Romulus, MI 48174
Phone: 734-729-4069
Toll-free: 800-837-0092
Fax: 800-860-0093
Internet: www.burgessinternational.com
E-mail: burgess@wwnet.com

Butler Ventamatic Corp.
HVAC
Wolters Industrial Park
Mineral Wells, TX 76067-0728
Phone: 940-325-7887
Toll-free: 800-433-1626
Fax: 940-325-9311
Internet: www.bvc.com
E-mail: bvc@bvc.com

C

Cabinet Studio
Cabinetry; Specialty Products
9709 Katy Fwy.
Houston, TX 77024
Phone: 713-461-6424
Toll-free: 800-761-6424
Fax: 713-461-0614
Internet: cabinetstudio.net
E-mail: calvin90@aol.com

Calorique Ltd.
HVAC; Landscaping & Outdoor Products
2380 Cranberry Hwy.
West Wareham, MA 02576
Phone: 508-291-4224
Fax: 508-291-2299
Internet: www.calorique.com
E-mail: heat@caloriq.ultranet.com

Canac Kitchens
Cabinetry
360 John St.
Thornhill, ON L3T 3M9 Canada
Phone: 905-881-2153
Toll-free: 800-CANAC-4U
Fax: 905-881-2392

Canital Granite
Countertops; Flooring
100 Hoka St.
Winnipeg, MB R2C 3N2
Canada
Phone: 204-224-2286
Toll-free: 800-665-0045
Fax: 204-222-8602

Canyon Creek Cabinet Co.
Cabinetry
16726 Tye St., S.E.
Monroe, WA 98272
Phone: 206-674-0800
Toll-free: 800-228-1830
Fax: 206-674-0998
Internet: www.
canyoncreek.com

Caradco
Windows & Glass
Part of the JELD-WEN family
201 Evans Rd.
P.O. Box 920
Rantoul, IL 61866
Phone: 217-893-4444
Toll-free: 800-238-1866
Fax: 800-225-9598
Internet: www.caradco.com
E-mail: caradco@aol.com

Cardiff Industries
Landscaping & Outdoor Products;
Windows & Glass
2428 N. Rose St.
Franklin Park, IL 60131
Phone: 847-455-3702
Toll-free: 800-349-8704
Fax: 847-455-3255
Internet: www.
cardiffindustries.com

Cardinal Homes, Inc.
Appliances; Cabinetry; Countertops;
Hardware; Plumbing, Faucets &
Fixtures; Structural Systems;
Windows & Glass
P.O. Box 10, Hwy. 15
Wylliesburg, VA 23976
Phone: 804-735-8111
Fax: 804-735-8824
Internet: www.
cardinalhomes.com
E-mail: cardinal@
cardinalhomes.com

The Carpet and Rug
Institute
Flooring
P.O. Box 2048
310 Holiday Ave.
Dalton, GA 30722-2048
Phone: 706-278-3176
Toll-free: 800-882-8846
Fax: 706-278-8835
Internet: www.carpet-rug.com

Casablanca Fan Co.
Electrical & Lighting
761 Corporate Center Dr.
Pomona, CA 91768
Phone: 909-629-1477
Toll-free: 888-227-2178
Fax: 909-629-0958

Ceilings & Interior Systems
Construction Assn.
Flooring; Walls, Finishes &
Insulation
1500 Lincoln Hwy.
Ste. 202
St. Charles, IL 60174
Phone: 630-584-1919
Toll-free: 800-524-7228
Fax: 630-584-2003
Internet: www.cisca.org

Central Brass
Plumbing, Faucets & Fixtures
2950 E. 55th St.
Cleveland, OH 44127
Phone: 216-883-0220
Toll-free: 800-321-8630
Fax: 800-338-9414

Central Lock and Hardware
Supply Co.
Cabinetry; Countertops; Doors—
Exterior; Doors—Interior; Electrical
& Lighting; Flooring; Garage
Doors, Openers & Accessories;
Hardware; Landscaping & Outdoor
Products; Plumbing, Faucets &
Fixtures; Specialty Products; Walls,
Finishes & Insulation
95 N.W. 166 St.
Miami, FL 33169
Phone: 305-947-4853
Toll-free: 800-677-4549
Fax: 305-949-8945

Centralite
Electrical & Lighting
6417 Hillcrest Park Ct.
Mobile, AL 36695
Phone: 334-607-9119
Toll-free: 877-466-5483
Fax: 334-607-9117
Internet: www.3mtech.com
E-mail: jimbusby@3mtech.com

CentralVac Intl.
Specialty Products
P.O. Box 160
1525 E. Fifth St.
Kimball, NE 69145
Phone: 308-235-4139
Toll-free: 800-666-3133
Fax: 308-235-4687
Internet: www.centralvac.com
E-mail: sales@centralvac.com

CertainTeed Corp.
Insulation Group
Walls, Finishes & Insulation
P.O. Box 860
Valley Forge, PA 19482-0860
Phone: 610-341-7739
Toll-free: 800-233-8990
Fax: 610-341-7571
Internet: www.certainteed.com
E-mail: tom.newton@ct.sgcna.
com

CertainTeed Corp. Pipe &
Plastics Group
Form-A-Drain and Outdoor
Living Designs
Landscaping & Outdoor Products;
Windows & Glass
P.O. Box 860
750 E. Swedesford Rd.
Valley Forge, PA 19482
Phone: 610-341-7000
Toll-free: 800-233-8990
Fax: 610-341-6837
Internet: www.certainteed.com
E-mail: ctoutdoor@certainteed.
com

Champagne Industries
Windows & Glass
12775 E. 38th Ave.
Denver, CO 80239
Phone: 303-375-0570
Toll-free: 800-375-5570
Fax: 303-375-1212
Internet: www.
champagneindustries.com
E-mail: lrs@dimensional.com

Chicago Faucets
Plumbing, Faucets & Fixtures
2100 Clearwater Dr.
Des Plaines, IL 60018-5999
Phone: 847-803-5000
Fax: 847-803-5454
Internet: www.chicagofaucets.
com

Circle Redmont
Flooring
2760 Business Center Blvd.
Melbourne, FL 32940
Phone: 407-259-7374
Toll-free: 800-358-3888
Fax: 407-259-7237
Internet: www.circleredmont.
com

Clever Solutions
Specialty Products
2122 Agincourt
Ann Arbor, MI 48103-5601
Phone: 734-668-2524
Fax: 734-668-2581
Internet: www.cleversolutions.
net
E-mail: sales@cleversolutions.
net

CMi Worldwide
Appliances; Electrical & Lighting
600 Stewart St., Suite 700
Seattle, WA 98101
Phone: 206-448-0354
Fax: 206-448-0359
Internet: www.
cmiworldwide.com
E-mail: info@cmiworldwide.
com

Columbia Forest Products
Flooring
222 S.W. Columbia
Ste. 1575
Portland, OR 97201
Phone: 503-224-5300
Fax: 503-224-5294
Internet: www.
columbiaforestproducts.com
E-mail: info@
columbiaforestproducts.com

Comtex Industries
Flooring
P.O. Box 802501
Aventura, FL 33280
Phone: 305-935-2965
Fax: 305-935-6344
E-mail: comtex@worldnet.att.
net

Concinnity
(A Div. of IW Industries)
Plumbing, Faucets & Fixtures;
Specialty Products
40 Melville Park Rd.
Melville, NY 11747
Phone: 516-293-7272
Toll-free: 800-356-9993
Fax: 516-293-3630
Internet: www.
concinnityusa.com

Congoleum Corp.
Flooring
P.O. Box 3127
Mercerville, NJ 08619
Phone: 609-584-3000
Fax: 609-584-3518
Internet: www.congoleum.com

Coni Marble Mfg.
Countertops; Plumbing, Faucets &
Fixtures
P.O. Box 40
Thorndale, ON N0M 2P0
Canada
Phone: 519-461-0100
Fax: 519-461-0733

Cool Attic
HVAC
Wolters Industrial Park
P.O. Box 670
Mineral Wells, TX 76068-0670
Phone: 940-325-7887
Toll-free: 800-433-1626
Fax: 940-325-9311
Internet: www.bvc.com
E-mail: bvc.com

CPFilms Inc.
Windows & Glass
P.O. Box 5068
Martinsville, VA 24115
Phone: 540-627-3000
Toll-free: 800-345-6088
Fax: 540-627-3032
Internet: www.vista-films.com

CPN, Inc.
Flooring
705 Moore Station
Industrial Park
Prospect Park, PA 19076
Toll-free: 800-437-3232
Fax: 610-534-2285
Internet: www.cpninc.com

Craft-Bilt Mfg. Co.
Landscaping & Outdoor Products
53 Souderton-Hatfield Pike
Souderton, PA 18964
Phone: 215-721-7700
Toll-free: 800-422-8577
Fax: 215-721-9338
Internet: www.craftbilt.com
E-mail: cbmross@aol.com

Crane Plumbing/Fiat
Products
Plumbing, Faucets & Fixtures

1235 Hartrey Ave.
Evanston, IL 60202
Phone: 847-864-7600
Fax: 847-864-7652
Internet: www.craneplumbing.
com

Create-A-Bed, C.A.B.
Specialty Products
5100 Preston Hwy.
Louisville, KY 40213
Phone: 502-966-3852
Toll-free: 877-966-3852
Fax: 502-966-4979
Internet: www.wallbed.com
E-mail: info@wallbed.com

Crossville Ceramics Co.
Countertops; Flooring
P.O. Box 1168
Crossville, TN 38557
Phone: 931-484-2110
Fax: 931-484-8418
Internet: www.
crossville-ceramics.com
E-mail: crossc@crossville.com

Curvoflite Stairs and
Millwork
Cabinetry
205 Spencer Ave.
Chelsea, MA 02150
Phone: 617-889-0007
Fax: 617-889-6339
Internet: www.curvoflite.com
E-mail: stairlady@cove.com

Custom Wood Products
Cabinetry; Specialty Products
P.O. Box 4500
Roanoke, VA 24015
Phone: 540-342-0363
Toll-free: 800-366-2971
Fax: 540-342-7789
Internet: www.cwp1.com
E-mail: cwp@roanoke.infi.net

D

d'ac Lighting
Electrical & Lighting
P.O. Box 262
Mamaroneck, NY 10543
Phone: 914-698-5959
Fax: 914-698-5577

Dakota Granite
Countertops; Flooring; Landscaping
& Outdoor Products
P.O. Box 1351
Milbank, SD 57252
Phone: 605-432-5580
Toll-free: 800-843-3333
Fax: 800-338-5346
Internet: www.dakgran.com
E-mail: dakota@dakgran.com

Dal-Tile Corp.
Flooring
7834 C.F. Hawn Fwy.
Dallas, TX 75217
Phone: 214-398-1411
Toll-free: 800-933-8453
Fax: 214-309-4457
Internet: www.daltile.com

Dalton Paradise Carpet
Flooring
P.O. Box 2488
Dalton, GA 30722
Phone: 706-226-9064
Toll-free: 800-338-7811
Fax: 706-226-9061

DEC-K-ING
Landscaping & Outdoor Products
P.O. Box 3929
Blaine, WA 98231
Toll-free: 800-804-6288
Fax: 604-530-4466
Internet: www.
globaldecking.com
E-mail: sales@dec-k-ing.com

Decorá
Cabinetry
1 Aristokraft Sq.
Jasper, IN 47547-0420
Phone: 812-634-2288
Fax: 812-634-2850
Internet: www.
decoracabinets.com

Decora Systems
Cabinetry; Specialty Products
P.O. Box 4504
Deerfield Beach, FL 33442
Phone: 954-425-8350
Fax: 954-425-8351

Defiant Safe Co.
Electrical & Lighting
3130 Towerwood Dr.
Dallas, TX 75234
Phone: 972-243-3711
Toll-free: 800-225-2984
Fax: 972-241-7669

Delaware Industries
Specialty Products
5649 Stow Rd.
Hudson, OH 44236
Phone: 330-655-2007
Toll-free: 800-450-6244
Fax: 330-655-2189
E-mail: delindinc@aol.com

Dependable Chemical Co.
Flooring
P.O. Box 16334
Rocky River, OH 44116-0334
Phone: 440-333-1123
Toll-free: 800-227-3434
Fax: 440-333-0070
Internet: www.floorprep.com
E-mail: dependable@
floorprep.com

Dietmeyer, Ward & Stroud
EnviroTech Radiant Fireplace
HVAC
P.O. Box 323
Vashon Island, WA 98070
Phone: 206-463-3722
Fax: 206-463-6335

Doorcraft
Part of the JELD-WEN family
Doors—Interior
3901 Cincinnati Ave.
Rocklin, CA 95765-1303
Phone: 916-782-4900
Toll-free: 800-877-9482
Internet: www.doors-windows.
com

Dorma Architectural Hardware
Doors—Exterior
Dorma Dr., Drawer AC
Reamstown, PA 17567-0411
Phone: 717-336-3881
Toll-free: 800-523-8483
Fax: 800-274-9724
Internet: www.dorma-usa.com
E-mail: mkt@dorma-usa.com

Dornbracht USA
Plumbing, Faucets & Fixtures
1750 Breckinridge Pkwy.
Ste. 510
Duluth, GA 30096
Toll-free: 800-774-1181
Fax: 800-899-8527
Internet: www.dornbracht.com
E-mail: dornbracht@
mindspring.com

Dura Supreme
Cabinetry
300 Dura Dr., P.O. Box K
Howard Lake, MN 55349
Phone: 320-543-3872
Fax: 320-543-3310

Dwyer Products Corp.
Appliances
418 N. Calumet
Michigan City, IN 46360-5019
Phone: 219-874-5236
Toll-free: 800-348-8508
Fax: 219-874-2823
Internet: www.
dwyerkitchens.com
E-mail: dwyerkit@mail.
netnitco.net

DYNASTY Range
Appliances
7355 E. Slauson Ave.
City of Commerce, CA 90040
Phone: 323-889-4888
Toll-free: 800-794-5233
Fax: 323-889-4890
Internet: www.dynastyrange.
com

E

Eagle Electric Mfg. Co.
Electrical & Lighting
45-31 Court Sq.
Long Island City, NY 11101
Phone: 718-937-8000
Toll-free: 800-441-3177
Fax: 718-482-0160
Internet: www.eagle-electric.
com

Eagle Window & Door
Windows & Glass
375 E. Ninth St.
P.O. Box 1072
Dubuque, IA 52004-1072
Phone: 319-556-2270
Toll-free: 800-453-3633
Fax: 319-556-4408
Internet: www.
eaglewindow.com
E-mail: eagleinc@
eaglewindow.com

Easy Heat
HVAC; Landscaping & Outdoor Products
31977 US 20 E.
New Carlisle, IN 46552
Toll-free: 800-537-4732
Internet: www.easyheat.com
E-mail: info@easyheat.com

E&E Consumer Products
Flooring
7200 Miller Dr.
Warren, MI 48092
Toll-free: 800-323-0982
Fax: 810-978-8400
E-mail: kenshore98@yahoo.
com

Electric Mirror
HVAC; Walls, Finishes & Insulation
P.O. Box 2426
Lynnwood, WA 98037
Phone: 425-787-0140
Toll-free: 888-218-9238
Fax: 425-787-1143
Internet: www.
electricmirror.com
E-mail: sales@
electricmirror.com

Eljer Plumbingware
Plumbing, Faucets & Fixtures
14801 Quorum Dr.
Dallas, TX 75240
Phone: 972-560-2000
Toll-free: 800-435-5372
Fax: 972-560-2269
Internet: www.eljer.com

Elkay Mfg. Co.
Plumbing, Faucets & Fixtures
2222 Camden Ct.
Oak Brook, IL 60523
Phone: 630-574-8484
Fax: 630-574-5012
Internet: www.elkay.com

Empire Comfort Systems
Appliances; Specialty Products
918 Freeburg Ave.
Belleville, IL 62222-0529
Phone: 618-233-7420
Toll-free: 800-851-3153
Fax: 618-233-7097
Internet: www.
empirecomfort.com
E-mail: empire@accessus.net

ENERJEE
HVAC
24 S. Lafayette Ave.
Morrisville, PA 19067
Phone: 215-295-0557
Fax: 215-736-2328
Internet: www.enerjee.com
E-mail: enerjee@enerjee.com

Enertel Controls
Electrical & Lighting; HVAC
2333 Wyecroft Rd., Unit 12
Oakville, ON L6L 6L4 Canada
Phone: 905-825-9441
Toll-free: 800-363-7835
Fax: 905-825-5492
Internet: www.enertel.com
E-mail: enertel@enertel.com

Enerzone Systems
(A Div. of Research Products Corp.)
HVAC
4103 Pecan Orchard
Parker, TX 75002
Phone: 972-424-9808
Toll-free: 888-STATNET
Fax: 972-424-8055
Internet: www.enerzone.com
E-mail: enerzone@airmail.net

Engelite Lighting
Electrical & Lighting
777 Richmond St. W.
Toronto, ON M6J 1C8 Canada
Phone: 416-504-5483
Fax: 416-504-5267
Internet: www.engelite.com
E-mail: info@engelite.com

Engineered Profiles
Div. of North American Profiles
Windows & Glass
7504-L 30th St. S.E.
Calgary, AB T2C 1M8 Canada
Phone: 403-279-4497
Toll-free: 877-436-3777
Fax: 800-979-4497
E-mail: epl@cadvision.com

Englert Inc.
Landscaping & Outdoor Products
1200 Amboy Ave.
P.O. Box 149
Perth Amboy, NJ 08862
Phone: 732-826-8614
Toll-free: 800-610-1975
Fax: 732-826-8865
Internet: www.englertinc.com
E-mail: englert.inc@cwixmail.
com

Everpure
Plumbing, Faucets & Fixtures
660 Blackhawk Dr.
Westmont, IL 60559
Phone: 630-654-4000
Toll-free: 800-323-7873
Fax: 630-654-1115
Internet: www.everpure.com
E-mail: info@everpure.com

Exeter Technologies, Inc.
Garage Doors, Openers & Accessories
One Penn Plaza
Suite 4025
New York, NY 10119
Phone: 212-760-0470
Toll-free: 888-393-8374
Fax: 212-760-0469
Internet: www.
park-zone or www.
exetertech.com
E-mail: info@park-zone.com

F

Fan America
HVAC
1748 Independence Blvd.
Ste. G-4
Sarasota, FL 34234
Phone: 941-359-3616
Toll-free: 800-838-4074
Fax: 941-359-3523
Internet: www.fanam.com
E-mail: nichefanam@
mindspring.com

Federal Home Products
Plumbing, Faucets & Fixtures
PO Box 1010
Ruston, LA 71273-1010
Phone: 318-255-5600
Toll-free: 800-637-6485
Fax: 318-255-5653

Feeny Mfg. Co.
Cabinetry; Specialty Products
P.O. Box 191
Muncie, IN 47308
Phone: 765-288-8730
Toll free: 800-899-6535
Fax: 765-288-0851
Internet: www.kv.com
E-mail: phil.sheridan@kv.com

Fiberez Bathware
Plumbing, Faucets & Fixtures
PO Box 295
Rooseveltown, NY 13683

Phone: 613-933-3525
Toll-free: 800-463-2779
Fax: 613-933-9844
E-mail: fiberez@glen-net.ca

Fieldstone Cabinetry
Cabinetry
P.O. Box 109
Northwood, IA 50459
Toll-free: 800-339-5369
Fax: 515-324-2390
Internet: www.
fieldstonecabinetry.com

Fillmore Thomas & Co.
Windows & Glass
350 County Center St.
P.O. Box 218
Lapeer, MI 48446
Phone: 810-664-2400
Toll-free: 800-482-6767
Fax: 800-488-9911
E-mail: tbwindow@tir.com

First Alert Professional Security Systems
Electrical & Lighting
175 Eileen Way
Syosset, NY 11791
Phone: 516-921-6066
Toll-free: 800-852-0086
Fax: 516-921-8118
Internet: www.firstalertpro.com

Fleetwood Homes
Structural Systems
3200 Myers St.
P.O. Box 7638
Riverside, CA 92513
Phone: 909-351-3500
Fax: 909-351-3697
Internet: www.fleetwood.com

Flos USA
Electrical & Lighting; Landscaping & Outdoor Products
200 McKay Rd.
Huntington Station, NY 11746
Phone: 516-549-2745
Fax: 516-549-4220

Folding Shutter Corp.
Windows & Glass
7089 Hemstreet Pl.
West Palm Beach, FL 33413
Phone: 407-683-4811
Fax: 407-640-8204
Internet: www.
foldingshutter.com
E-mail: mail@foldingshutter.
com

Forbo Industries
Flooring
Humboldt Industrial Park
P.O. Box 667
Hazleton, PA 18201
Phone: 717-459-0771
Toll-free: 800-342-0604
Fax: 717-450-0258

Formica Corp.
Countertops; Flooring
10155 Reading Rd.
Cincinnati, OH 45241-4805
Phone: 513-786-3400
Toll-free: 800-FORMICA
Fax: 513-786-3024
Internet: www.formica.com

Four Seasons Sunrooms
Structural Systems
5005 Veterans Memorial Hwy.
Holbrook, NY 11741
Toll-free: 800-FOUR SEASONS
Fax: 516-563-4010
Internet: www.
four-seasons-sunrooms.com

Franke Consumer Products
Kitchen Systems Div.
Appliances; Plumbing, Faucets & Fixtures
3050 Campus Dr., Ste. 500
Hatfield, PA 19440
Toll-free: 800-626-5771
Fax: 215-822-5873
Internet: www.franke.com/ksd

Manufacturers & Suppliers Index

Franklin Brass Mfg. Co.
Specialty Products
P.O. Box 4887
Carson, CA 90749-4887
Phone: 310-885-3200
Toll-free: 800-421-3375
Fax: 310-885-5739
Internet: www.
franklinbrass.com
E-mail: darryls@
franklinbrass.com

**Friedrich Air
Conditioning Co.**
HVAC
P.O. Box 1540
San Antonio, TX 78295
Phone: 210-357-4400
Toll-free: 800-541-6645
Fax: 210-357-4480
Internet: www.friedrich.com
E-mail: hvac@friedrich.com

Frontier Access & Mobility
*Specialty Products; Structural
Systems*
4000 Central Ave. No. 4
Cheyenne, WY 82001-1329
Phone: 307-637-7663
Toll-free: 800-868-7663
Fax: 307-637-7745

Fypon
Walls, Finishes & Insulation
22 W. Pennsylvania Ave.
P.O. Box 365
Stewartstown, PA 17363
Phone: 717-993-2593
Toll-free: 800-537-5349
Fax: 717-993-3782
Internet: www.fypon.com

G

GE Appliances
Appliances
Appliance Park
Louisville, KY 40225
Phone: 502-452-0383
Toll-free: 800-626-2000
Fax: 502-452-0383
Internet: www.geappliances.
com

GE Company
GE Lighting
Electrical & Lighting
Nela Park
Cleveland, OH 44112
Phone: 216-266-2053
Toll-free: 800-GE-LAMPS
Fax: 804-965-1022
Internet: www.ge.com

Geberit Mfg.
Plumbing, Faucets & Fixtures
1100 Boone Dr.
Michigan City, IN 46360-7730
Toll-free: 800-225-7217
Fax: 219-872-8003

**Gemini Bath &
Kitchen Products**
Plumbing, Faucets & Fixtures
1501 E. Broadway
P.O. Box 43398
Tucson, AZ 85733-3398
Phone: 520-770-0667
Fax: 520-770-9964
Internet: www.geminibkp.com
E-mail: geminibkp@geminibkp.
com

General Ecology
Plumbing, Faucets & Fixtures
151 Sheree Blvd.
Exton, PA 19341
Phone: 610-363-7900
Toll-free: 800-441-8166
Fax: 610-363-0412
Internet: www.
generalecology.com
E-mail: info@
generalecology.com

General Shale Brick
Landscaping & Outdoor Products
P.O. Box 3547
Johnson City, TN 37602
Phone: 423-282-4661
Toll-free: 800-414-4661
Fax: 423-952-4104
Internet: www.
generalshale.com

**Gerber Plumbing Fixtures
Corp.**
Plumbing, Faucets & Fixtures
4600 W. Touhy Ave.
Chicago, IL 60646
Phone: 847-675-6570
Fax: 800-5-GERBER (except IL)
Internet: www.gerberonline.
com

Gibco Services
*Cabinetry; Flooring; Walls, Finishes
& Insulation*
725 S. Adams Rd.
Ste. L-59
Birmingham, MI 48009
Phone: 248-647-3322
Fax: 248-647-8720

GINGER/GUSA
*Electrical & Lighting; Specialty
Products; Walls, Finishes &
Insulation*
460-N Greenway Industrial Dr.
Ft. Mill, SC 29708
Phone: 803-547-5786
Toll-free: 800-842-4872
Fax: 803-547-6356
E-mail: info@gingerco.com

Glen Oak Lumber & Milling
Flooring
N2885 County F
Montello, WI 53949-9012
Phone: 608-297-2161
Toll-free: 800-242-8272
ext. 233
Fax: 608-297-7651
Internet: www.
glenoaklumber.com

Globe Fire Sprinkler Corp.
Electrical & Lighting
4077 Air Park Dr.
Standish, MI 48658
Phone: 517-846-4583
Toll-free: 800-248-0278
Fax: 517-846-9231
Internet: www.
globesprinkler.com
E-mail: globe_man@msn.com

Gorell Enterprises
Windows & Glass
1380 Wayne Ave.
Indiana, PA 15701
Phone: 724-465-1800
Fax: 724-465-1894
Internet: www.gorell.com
E-mail: info@gorell.com

Gothic Arch Greenhouses
(A Div. of Trans-Sphere
Trading Corp.)
Structural Systems
P.O. Box 1564
Mobile, AL 36633
Phone: 334-432-7529
Toll-free: 800-628-4974

Grass America
Cabinetry
P.O. Box 1019
1202 Hwy. 66 S.
Kernersville, NC 27284
Phone: 336-996-4041
Toll-free: 800-334-3512
Fax: 336-996-5149
Internet: www.grassusa.com
E-mail: info@grassusa.com

Great Lakes Plastics
Plumbing, Faucets & Fixtures
501 W. Lawson St.
St. Paul, MN 55117
Phone: 651-487-4897
Toll-free: 800-999-6077
Fax: 651-487-4878
Internet: www.warmrain.com
E-mail: tedk@warmrain.com

Great Lakes Window
Windows & Glass
P.O. Box 1896
Toledo, OH 43603-1896
Phone: 419-666-5555
Toll-free: 800-666-0000
Fax: 419-661-2926
Internet: www.
greatlakeswindow.com
E-mail: webmaster@
greatlakeswindow.com

GTE Corp.
Electrical & Lighting
532 LaGuardia Pl.
Ste. 234
New York, NY 10012
Toll-free: 800-828-7280
Fax: 972-507-5002
Internet: www.gte.com

H

Hafele America
*Cabinetry; Countertops; Doors—
Interior; Electrical & Lighting;
Hardware; Specialty Products*
3901 Cheyenne Dr.
P.O. Box 4000
Archdale, NC 27263
Phone: 336-889-2322
Toll-free: 800-423-3531
Fax: 336-431-3831
Internet: www.hafeleus.com

Halo Lighting
(A Brand of Cooper Lighting)
Electrical & Lighting
400 Busse Rd.
Elk Grove Village, IL 60007
Phone: 847-956-8400
Fax: 847-806-3980

Hanover Lantern
Landscaping & Outdoor Products
350 King La.
Hanover, PA 17331-1733
Phone: 717-632-6464
Fax: 717-632-5039
Internet: www.
hanoverlantern.com
E-mail: hanoverlantern@
sun-link.com

Harrington Brass Works
Plumbing, Faucets & Fixtures
7 Pearl Ct.
Allendale, NJ 07401
Phone: 201-818-1300
Fax: 201-818-0099

Harris-Tarkett, Inc.
Flooring
P.O. Box 300
2225 Eddie Williams Rd.
Johnson City, TN 37605-0300
Phone: 423-928-3122
Toll-free: 800-842-7816
Fax: 423-928-9445
Internet: www.
harris-tarkett.com

Hartco Flooring Co.
An Armstrong Company
Flooring
16803 Dallas Pkwy.
Addison, TX 75001
Phone: 214-887-2100
Toll-free: 800-442-7826
Fax: 214-887-2234
Internet: www.hartcoflooring.
com

Hartford Conservatories
*Doors—Exterior; Doors—Interior;
Structural Systems; Windows
& Glass*
96A Commerce Way
Woburn, MA 01801
Phone: 781-937-9050
Toll-free: 800-963-8700
Fax: 781-937-9025
Internet: www.
hartford~con.com
E-mail: hartford@
hartford~con.com

**Hayfield Window &
Door Co.**
Windows & Glass
P.O. Box 25
Industrial Park Rd.
Hayfield, MN 55940
Phone: 507-477-3224
Fax: 507-477-3605

H.B. Ives
*Hardware; Plumbing, Faucets &
Fixtures*
62 Barnes Park Rd. N.
Wallingford, CT 06492
Phone: 203-294-4837
Fax: 203-284-1460

HDI
Cabinetry
107 Mill Plain Rd.
Danbury, CT 06811
Phone: 203-743-5161
Toll-free: 800-431-1904
Fax: 203-797-1528
Internet: www.
drawerslides.com
E-mail: hdi@drawerslides.com

Heat Controller
HVAC
1900 Wellworth Ave.
Jackson, MI 49203
Phone: 517-787-2100
Fax: 517-787-9341

**Heat-N-Glo Fireplace
Products**
Specialty Products
20802 Kensington Blvd.
Lakeville, MN 55044
Phone: 612-985-6000
Toll-free: 888-427-3973
Fax: 612-985-6001
Internet: www.heatnglo.com

Heatway
Electrical & Lighting; HVAC
3131 W. Chestnut Expwy.
Springfield, MO 65802
Phone: 417-864-6108
Toll-free: 800-255-1996
Fax: 417-864-8161
Internet: www.heatway.com

The Hess Mfg. Co.
Doors—Exterior; Windows & Glass
P.O. Box 127
Quincy, PA 17247-0127
Phone: 717-749-3141
Toll-free: 800-541-6666
Fax: 717-749-3712
Internet: www.armaclad.com
E-mail: armaclad@cvn.net

.hessamerica
Landscaping & Outdoor Products
639 Washburn Switch Rd.
Shelby, NC 28151
Phone: 704-471-2211
Fax: 704-471-2255
Internet: www.hessamerica.com

Holiday Kitchens
(A Div. of Mastercraft
Industries)
Cabinetry
120 W. Allen St.
Rice Lake, WI 54868
Phone: 715-234-8111
Fax: 715-234-6370

Home Crest Corp.
Cabinetry
1002 Eisenhower Dr. N.
P.O. Box 595
Goshen, IN 46526
Phone: 219-535-9300
Fax: 800-737-1500
Internet: www.
homecrestcab.com
E-mail: hcinfo@
homecrestcab.com

The Home Store
Structural Systems
73 State Rd., P.O. Box 300
Whately, MA 01093
Phone: 413-665-1266
Toll-free: 800-974-1266 (New
England)
Fax: 413-665-1122
Internet: www.
the-homestore.com

**Honeywell Home &
Building Control**
Electrical & Lighting; HVAC
2701 4th Ave. S.
Minneapolis, MN 55408
Phone: 800-441-7017
Fax: 612-951-2086
Internet: www.honeywell.com.

Horton Automatics
Doors—Exterior
4242 Baldwin Blvd.
Corpus Christi, TX 78405
Phone: 361-888-5591
Toll-free: 800-531-3111
Fax: 361-888-6510

Internet: www.
hortondoors.com
E-mail: aida_guzman@
overheaddoor.com

Hoyme Mfg.
HVAC
3843 44 Ave.
Camrose, AB T4V 3T1 Canada
Phone: 780-672-6553
Toll-free: 800-661-7382
Fax: 800-661-8065

Hubbell Lighting
*Electrical & Lighting; Landscaping
& Outdoor Products*
2000 Electric Way
Christiansburg, VA 24073-2500
Phone: 540-382-6111
Fax: 540-382-1526
Internet: www.hubbell-ltg.com

Hunter Technology
Appliances; Specialty Products
P.O. Box 400
Orillia, ON L3V 6K1 Canada
Phone: 705-325-6111
Fax: 705-327-5658
Internet: www.
huntertechnology.com
E-mail: hunter-energy@
encode.com

Hurd Millwork Co.
Windows & Glass
575 S. Whelen Ave.
Medford, WI 54451
Phone: 715-748-2011
Toll-free: 800-433-4873
Fax: 715-748-6043
Internet: www.hurd.com

Huron Window Corp.
Doors—Exterior; Windows & Glass
345 Mountain St. S.
Morden, MB R6M 1J5 Canada
Phone: 204-822-6281
Toll-free: 800-565-3493
Fax: 204-822-6343
Internet: www.huronwin.com
E-mail: huron@huronwin.com

H-Window Company
Windows & Glass
1324 E. Oakwood Dr.
Monticello, MN 55362
Phone: 612-295-5305
Fax: 612-295-4656
Internet: www.h-window.com
E-mail: hway@h-window.com

I

Idaho Wood
Landscaping & Outdoor Products
P.O. Box 488
Sandpoint, ID 83864
Phone: 208-263-9521
Toll-free: 800-635-1100
Fax: 208-263-3102

**Independent Living
Aids, Inc.**
*Appliances; Electrical & Lighting;
HVAC*
27 E. Mall
Plainview, NY 11803
Phone: 516-752-8080
Toll-free: 800-537-2118
Fax: 516-572-3135
Internet: www.
independentliving.com
E-mail: can-do@
independentliving.com

Insulate Windows
Windows & Glass
5001 D St., N.W.
Auburn, WA 98001
Phone: 253-850-9000
Toll-free: 800-227-3699
Fax: 800-645-6253
Internet: www.insulate.com

IntelliNct
Electrical & Lighting; HVAC
2900 Horseshoe Dr. S.
Naples, FL 34104
Phone: 941-434-5888
Toll-free: 800-899-1372
Fax: 941-434-8429
Internet: www.
intellinetcontrols.com
E-mail: intellinet@
worldnet.att.net

Interceramic, USA
Countertops; Flooring
2333 S. Jupiter Rd.
Garland, TX 75041
Phone: 214-503-5500
Toll free: 800 496-8453
Fax: 214-503-5575
Internet: www.interceramicusa.
com

International Paper Co.
Doors—Interior
2 Manhattanville Rd.
Purchase, NY 10577
Phone: 914-397-1500
Toll-free: 800-223-1268
Fax: 914-397-1650
Internet: www.
internationalpaper.com
E-mail: comm@ipaper.com

**International
Window/Maestro**
Doors—Exterior
5625 E. Firestone Blvd.
South Gate, CA 90280
Phone: 562-928-6411
Fax: 562-928-3492
Internet: www.intlwindow.com

IRON-A-WAY
Specialty Products
220 W. Jackson
Morton, IL 61550-1588
Phone: 309-266-7232
Fax: 309-266-5088
Internet: www.ironaway.com
E-mail: ironaway@
ironaway.com

ISTEC Corp.
HVAC
415 Hope Ave.
P.O. Box 618
Roselle, NJ 07203
Phone: 908-241-8880
Fax: 908-241-7288
Internet: www.istec-corp.com
E-mail: sales@istec-corp.com

**Italian Trade Commission,
Tile Center**
Flooring
499 Park Ave., Sixth Fl.
New York, NY 10022
Phone: 212-980-1500
Fax: 212-758-1050
Internet: www.italytile.com
E-mail: newyork@italtrade.com

IXL Cabinets
(A Div. of Triangle Pacific)
Cabinetry
16803 Dallas Pkwy.
Addison, TX 75001
Phone: 214-887-2000
Toll-free: 800-527-5903
Fax: 800-527-5903, ext.434
Internet: www.ixlcabinets.com
E-mail: info@ixlcabinets.com

J

Jackson Medical Equipment
*Hardware; HVAC; Plumbing,
Faucets & Fixtures; Specialty
Products; Structural Systems*
982 Thomas Ave.
St. Paul, MN 55104-2638
Phone: 651-645-6221

Jacuzzi Whirlpool Bath
Plumbing, Faucets & Fixtures
P.O. Drawer J
2121 N. California Blvd.
Ste. 475
Walnut Creek, CA 94596
Phone: 925-938-7070
Toll-free: 800-288-4002
Fax: 925-938-3025
Internet: www.jacuzzi.com
E-mail: info@jacuzzi.com

**JADO Bathroom &
Hardware Mfg. Corp.**
*Hardware; Plumbing, Faucets &
Fixtures*
7845 E. Paradise Ln.
Scottsdale, AZ 85260-1797
Phone: 480-951-2675
Fax: 800-552-5236

Jason Intl.
Plumbing, Faucets & Fixtures
8328 MacArthur Dr.
North Little Rock, AR 72118
Phone: 501-771-4477
Toll-free: 800-255-5766
Fax: 501-771-2333
Internet: www.jasonint.com
E-mail: mktg@jasonint.com

Jenn-Air
Appliances
403 W. Fourth St. North
Newton, IA 50208
Toll-free: 800-JENN-AIR
Internet: www.jennair.com

Jensen Medical
*Doors—Exterior; Plumbing,
Faucets & Fixtures; Specialty
Products; Structural Systems*
1900 S. Quince St. No. A
Denver, CO 80231-3232
Phone: 303-751-7292

Just Mfg. Co.
Plumbing, Faucets & Fixtures
9233 King St.
Franklin Park, Il 60131
Phone: 847-678-5150
Fax: 847-678-6817
Internet: www.justsinks.com
E-mail: justsinkswwz.com

K

Kanalflakt
Appliances
50 Sheridan Rd.
P.O. Box 2000
Bouctouche, NB E0A 1G0
Canada
Phone: 506-743-9500
Fax: 506-743-9600
Internet: www.kanalflakt.com
E-mail: male@kanalflakt.com

Kaycan
*Doors—Exterior; Landscaping &
Outdoor Products; Windows
& Glass*
402 Boyer Cir.
Williston, VT 05495
Phone: 802-865-0114
Toll free: 800 952 9226
Fax: 802-865-0268
Internet: www.kaycan.com

Kentucky Wood Floors
Flooring
P.O. Box 33276
Louisville, KY 40232
Phone: 502-451-6024
Toll-free: 800-235-5235
Fax: 502-451-6027
Internet: www.
kentuckywood.com
E-mail: jstern@
kentuckywood.com

Kepcor/SSI Tiles
Countertops; Flooring
P.O. Box 119
Minerva, OH 44657
Phone: 330-868-6434
Fax: 330-868-6437

Kidde Fyrnetics
Electrical & Lighting
1055 Stevenson Ct.
#102W
Roselle, IL 60172
Phone: 630-893-4592
Toll-free: 800-654-7665
Fax: 630-893-9967
E-mail: kfetzer@kidde.com

Kinetico
Plumbing, Faucets & Fixtures
10845 Kinsman Rd.
P.O. Box 193
Newbury, OH 44065
Phone: 440-564-9111
Toll-free: 800-944-9283
Fax: 440-564-9541
Internet: www.kinetico.com
E-mail: custserv@kinetico.com

Kohler Co.
*Cabinetry; Plumbing, Faucets &
Fixtures*
444 Highland Dr.
Kohler, WI 53044

Phone: 920-457-4441
Toll-free: 800-4KOHLER
Fax: 920-457-1271
Internet: www.kohlerco.com

Kolbe & Kolbe Millwork Co.
Doors—Exterior; Windows & Glass
1323 S. 11th Ave.
Wausau, WI 54401-5998
Phone: 715-842-5666
Toll-free: 800-955-8177
Fax: 715-845-8270
Internet: www.kolbe-kolbe.com
E-mail: kolbe@kolbe-kolbe.com

Kolson
*Cabinetry; Hardware; Landscaping
& Outdoor Products; Plumbing,
Faucets & Fixtures*
653 Middle Neck Rd.
Great Neck, NY 11023
Phone: 516-487-1224
Toll-free: 800-783-1335
Fax: 516-487-1231
Internet: www.kolson.com
E-mail: kolson1@idt.net

Kool-O-Matic Corp.
HVAC
P.O. Box 310
Niles, MI 49120
Phone: 616-683-2600
Fax: 616-683-2318

KraftMaid Cabinetry
Cabinetry
P.O. Box 1055
15535 S. State Ave.
Middlefield, OH 44062
Phone: 440-632-5333
Toll-free: 800-571-1990
Fax: 440-632-5648
Internet: www.kraftmaid.com
E-mail: sales@kraftmaid.com

Kuehn Bevel
Countertops
111 Canfield Ave.
Randolph, NJ 07869
Phone: 973-584-8282
Toll-free: 800-TO-BEVEL
Fax: 973-584-1855
Internet: www.kuehnbevel.com
E-mail: kuehnbevel@
worldnet.att.net

KWC Faucets
Plumbing, Faucets & Fixtures
1555 Oakbrook Dr.
No. 110
Norcross, GA 30093
Phone: 770-248-1600
Toll-free: 888-KWC-FCTS
Fax: 888-FAX-KWC1
Internet: www.kwcfaucets.com

L

L. B. Plastics
Landscaping & Outdoor Products
482 E. Plaza Dr.
P.O. Box 907
Mooresville, NC 28115
Phone: 704-663-1543
Toll-free: 800-752-7739
Fax: 704-664-2989

**Lamson-Taylor Custom
Doors**
Doors—Exterior
Tucker Rd.
S. Acworth, NH 03607
Phone: 603-835-2992
Fax: 603-835-2992

Lasco Bathware
(A Div. of Tomkins Industries)
Plumbing, Faucets & Fixtures
3255 E. Miraloma Ave.
Anaheim, CA 92806
Phone: 714-993-1220
Toll-free: 800-877-2005
Fax: 714-528-1161
Internet: www.lascobathware.
com

Latco Products
Countertops; Flooring
13536 Saticoy St.
Van Nuys, CA 91402
Phone: 818-902-5424
Fax: 818-902-5434
Internet: latcotile@earthlink.net

LDBrinkman
Flooring
1655 Waters Ridge Dr.
Lewisville, TX 75057
Phone: 972-353-3500
Fax: 972-353-3621

Ledco
Doors—Interior
801 Commerce Cir.
Shelbyville, KY 40065
Phone: 502-633-6304
Toll-free: 800-626-6367
Fax: 502-633-6461

Lee/Rowan Co.
Building Products Div.
Specialty Products
900 S. Hwy. Dr.
Fenton, MO 63026
Phone: 314-343-0700
Toll-free: 800-325-6150
Fax: 314-349-9618
Internet: www.leerowan.com

Leonard Valve Co.
Plumbing, Faucets & Fixtures
1360 Elmwood Ave.
Cranston, RI 02910-3824
Phone: 401-461-1200
Fax: 401-941-5310
Internet: www.
leonardvalve.com
E-mail: info@leonardvalve.com

LesCare Kitchens
Cabinetry
1 LesCare Dr.
Waterbury, CT 06705
Phone: 203-755-1100
Fax: 203-755-4713
Internet: www.
lescarekitchens.com
E-mail: survey@
lescarekitchens.com

Leviton Mfg.
*Electrical & Lighting; HVAC;
Landscaping and Outdoor Products*
59-25 Little Neck Pkwy..
Little Neck, NY 11362
Phone: 718-229-4040
Fax: 800-U-FAX-LEV
Internet: www.leviton.com

Lifetime Faucets
Plumbing, Faucets & Fixtures
PO Box 2820
301 Mid-America Blvd.
Hot Springs, AR 71913
Phone: 501-760-1140
Toll-free: 800-238-7558
Fax: 501-760-1565
Internet: www.direclynx.
net/~lifetime
E-mail: spensko@direclynx.net

Lift Aid
Specialty Products
38281 Schoolcraft Rd.
Suite B
Livonia, MI 48150-5000
Phone: 734-432-9500
Toll-free: 800-951-4243
Fax: 734-432-0098
Internet: www.liftaid.com

Lighting Services
Electrical & Lighting
2 Kay Fries Dr.
Stony Point, NY 10980
Phone: 914-942-2800
Toll-free: 800-999-9574
Fax: 914-942-2177
Internet: www.
lightingservicesinc.com

Lightway Industries
Electrical & Lighting
28435 Industry Dr.
Valencia, CA 91355
Phone: 805-257-0286
Toll-free: 800-325-4448
Fax: 805-257-0201
Internet: www.lightwayind.com
E-mail: info@lightwayind.com

Lippert Corp.
Plumbing, Faucets & Fixtures
P.O. Box 1030, W142 N8999
Fountain Blvd.
Menomonee Falls, WI
53052-1030
Phone: 414-255-2350

Toll-free: 800-869-8775
Fax: 414-255-2304

**Lodestar
Statements in Stone**
Countertops
231 E. 58th St.
New York, NY 10022
Phone: 212-755-1818
Fax: 212-755-1828

**Logcrafters Log & Timber
Homes**
*Doors—Exterior; Doors—Interior;
Windows & Glass*
P.O. Box 448
St. Ignatius, MT 59865
Phone: 406-745-3482
Toll-free: 800-735-4425
Fax: 406-745-3350
Internet: www.logcrafter.com
E-mail: logcraft@logcrafter.com

London Tile Co.
Flooring
65 Walnut St.
New London, OH 44851
Phone: 419-929-1551
Toll-free: 888-757-1551
Fax: 419-929-1552

LTS Ceramics
Countertops; Flooring
1224 Bell Ave.
Ft. Pierce, FL 34982-6582
Phone: 561-465-5445
Fax: 561-465-4553
Internet: www.LtsCeramics.com
E-mail: ltstile@aol.com

Lubidet USA
Plumbing, Faucets & Fixtures
1980 S. Quebec St., No. 4
Denver, CO 80231
Phone: 303-368-4555
Toll-free: 800-582-4338
Fax: 303-368-0812
Internet: www.lubidet.com
E-mail: info@lubidet.com

Luxo Corp.
Electrical & Lighting
36 Midland Ave.
P.O. Box 951
Port Chester, NY 10573
Phone: 914-937-4433
Fax: 914-937-7016

Lyons Industries
Plumbing, Faucets & Fixtures
30,000-M-62W.
Dowagiac, MI 49047
Phone: 616-782-3404
Toll-free: 800-458-9036
Fax: 616-782-5159

M

M & S Systems
*Electrical & Lighting; Specialty
Products*
2861 Congressman Ln.
Dallas, TX 75220
Phone: 214-358-3196
Toll-free: 800-877-6631
Fax: 214-350-1913
Internet: www.mssystems.com
E-mail: rpinell@mssystems.com

MAAX
Plumbing, Faucets & Fixtures
600 Rt. Cameron
Ste-Marie, PQ G6E 1B2 Canada
Phone: 418-387-4155
Toll-free: 800-463-6229
Fax: 418-387-3507
Internet: www.maax.com

**Malta Wood Windows
& Doors**
Windows & Glass
(A Div. of Tompkins)
P.O. Box 397, 13th St.
Malta, OH 43758
Phone: 614-962-3131
Toll-free: 800-727-5167
Fax: 614-962-3700

Mannington Mills
Flooring
P.O. Box 30
Salem, NJ 08079
Phone: 609-339-5848
Fax: 609-339-5948

Internet: www.mannington.
com
E-mail: jimc3@mannington.
com

**Mansfield Plumbing
Products**
Plumbing, Faucets & Fixtures
1070 Polaris Pkwy.
Suite 200
Columbus, OH 43240
Phone: 614-825-0960
Fax: 614-825-0989
Internet: www.
mansfieldplumbing.com
E-mail: custserv@
mansfieldplumbing.com

Marquis Carpet Mills
Flooring
2743 Hwy. 76
P.O. Box 1308
Chatsworth, GA 30705
Phone: 706-695-1060
Toll-free: 800-609-3100
Fax: 706-695-4787

Marsh Furniture Co.
Cabinetry
P.O. Box 870
High Point, NC 27261-0870
Phone: 336-884-7363
Fax: 336-884-0883
Internet: www.
marshfurniture.com

Martin Door Mfg.
*Garage Doors, Openers &
Accessories*
2828 S. 900 W.
P.O. Box 27437
Salt Lake City, UT 84127-0437
Phone: 801-973-9310
Toll-free: 800-388-9310
Fax: 801-977-4222
Internet: www.martindoor.com

Marvel Industries
Appliances
P.O. Box 997
Richmond, IN 47375
Phone: 765-962-2521
Toll-free: 800-428-6644
Fax: 765-962-2493
Internet: www.
marvelindustries.com

Mason Corp.
Structural Systems
P.O. Box 59226
Birmingham, AL 35259-9226
Phone: 205-942-4100
Toll-free: 800-868-4100
Fax: 205-945-4399

Masonite Corp.
Doors—Interior
1 S. Wacker Dr., Ste. 3600
Chicago, IL 60606
Phone: 312-750-0900
Toll-free: 800-255-0785
Fax: 312-750-1233
Internet: www.masonite.com
E-mail: jerry.hills@ipaper.com

Matot
Specialty Products
2501 Van Buren
Bellwood, IL 60104-2459
Phone: 708-547-1888
Toll-free: 800-369-1070
Fax: 708-547-1608
Internet: www.matot.com
E-mail: sales@matot.com

Maxxon Corp.
(formerly Gyp-Crete Corp.)
HVAC
920 Hamel Rd.
Hamel, MN 55340
Phone: 612-478-9600
Toll-free: 800-356-7887
Fax: 612-478-2431
Internet: www.maxxon.com
E-mail: info@maxxon.com

Mayse Woodworking Co.
Flooring
319 Richardson Rd.
Lansdale, PA 19446
Phone: 215-822-8307
Toll-free: 888-LONGLEAF
Fax: 215-822-8307

Medically Yours
*Plumbing, Faucets & Fixtures;
Specialty Products*
3839 Merle Hay Rd.
No. 170
Des Moines, IA 50310-1320
Phone: 515-270-0725
Fax: 515-270-0166
E-mail: medyours@aol.com

Metals USA-National Mfg.
*Structural Systems; Windows
& Glass*
811 Atlantic
North Kansas City, MO
64116-3918
Phone: 816-221-8990
Toll-free: 800-444-9978
Fax: 816-221-8990
Internet: www.metalsusa.com
E-mail: natpatio@aol.com

Metropolitan Ceramics
Flooring
P.O. Box 9240
Canton, OH 44711
Phone: 330-484-4887
Toll-free: 800-325-3945
Fax: 330-484-4880
Internet: www.
metroceramics.com
E-mail: info@
ironrockcapital.com

**Meyer Enterprises/
Insul-Tray**
Walls, Finishes & Insulation
456 Camp St.
E. Peoria, IL 61611
Phone: 309-698-0062
Toll-free: 800-266-8410,
800-236-6107
Fax: 309-698-0065

Miami-Carey Ltd.
Electrical & Lighting; HVAC
P.O. Box 41524
230 Sandalwood Pkwy.
Brampton, ON L6Z 4R1 Canada
Phone: 905-840-5396
Toll-free: 800-561-0749
Fax: 905-840-5711
E-mail: mr.whisper@
sympatico.ca

Mid Continent Cabinetry
(A Div. of Norcraft Cos.)
Cabinetry
3020 Denmark Ave.
Ste. 100
Eagan, MN 55121
Phone: 651-234-3300
Fax: 651-234-3398
Internet: www.
midcontinentcabinetry.com

Miele Inc.
Appliances
9 Independence Way
Princeton, NJ 08540
Phone: 609-419-9898
Toll-free: 800-843-7231
Fax: 609-419-4298
Internet: www.mieleusa.com

Mirolin Industries
Plumbing, Faucets & Fixtures
60 Shorncliffe Rd.
Toronto, ON M8Z 5K1 Canada
Phone: 416-231-9030
Toll-free: 800-MIROLIN
Fax: 416-231-0929
E-mail: mirolin@aol.com

Modular Hardware
Hardware; Specialty Products
8190 N. Brookshire Ct.
P.O. Box 35398
Tucson, AZ 85740
Toll-free: 800-533-0042
Fax: 800-533-7942
Internet: www.
modularhardware.com
E-mail: modhdwe@
modhdwe.com

Moen
Plumbing, Faucets & Fixtures
25300 Al Moen Dr.
North Olmsted, OH 44070-8022
Phone: 440-962-2000
Toll-free: 800-289-6636
Fax: 440-962-2770

Manufacturers & Suppliers Index

Phifer Wire Products
Windows & Glass
P.O. Box 1700
Tuscaloosa, AL 35403-1700
Phone: 205-345-2120
Toll-free: 800-633-5955
Fax: 205-750-3041
Internet: www.phifer.com
E-mail: phiferad@dbtech.net

Pivitol Suspension Seating
Structural Systems
341 W. 1185 North
Orem, UT 84057
Phone: 801-724-9896
Toll-free: 800-678-7328
Fax: 801-225-0910
Internet: www.pivotal-seating.com

Plain & Fancy Custom Cabinetry
Cabinetry
P.O. Box 519
Rt. 501 and Oak St.
Schaefferstown, PA 17088-0519
Phone: 717-949-6571
Toll-free: 800-447-9006
Fax: 717-949-2114
Internet: www.homeportfolio.com
E-mail: pfcustcab@desupernet.net

Playworld Systems, Inc.
Structural Systems
1000 Buffalo Rd.
Lewisburg, PA 17837
Phone: 570-522-9800
Toll-free: 800-233-8404
Fax: 570-522-3030
Internet: www.playworldsystems.com
E-mail: webmaster@playworldsystems.com

Plaza Hardwood
Flooring
219 W. Manhattan Ave.
Santa Fe, NM 87501
Phone: 505-992-3260
Toll-free: 800-662-6306
Fax: 505-992-8766
Internet: www.plzfloor.com
E-mail: paulfuge@plzfloor.com

Point Electric
Electrical & Lighting
P.O. Box 619
Nanuet, NY 10954-0619
Phone: 914-623-3471
Fax: 914-623-1861
E-mail: swivelier@juno.com

Polymer Plastics Corp.
Flooring; Landscaping & Outdoor Products; Walls, Finishes & Insulation
65 Davids Dr.
Hauppauge, NY 11788
Phone: 516-231-1300
Toll-free: 800-777-6596
Fax: 516-231-1329
E-mail: vturf@aol.com

Poly-Tak Protection Systems
Walls, Finishes & Insulation; Windows & Glass
5731 McFadden Ave.
Huntington Beach, CA 92649
Phone: 714-892-6128
Toll-free: 800-899-0871
Fax: 714-892-7128
Internet: www.polytak.com
E-mail: polytak@earthlink.net

Power Access Corp.
Doors—Exterior; Doors—Interior
106 Powder Mill Rd.
Collinsville, CT 06022
Phone: 860-693-0751
Toll-free: 800-344-0088
Fax: 860-693-0641
Internet: www.power-access.com
E-mail: s/s@power-access.com

Precision Multiple Controls
Electrical & Lighting
33 Greenwood Ave.
Midland Park, NJ 07432
Phone: 201-444-0600
Fax: 201-444-8575

Internet: www.precisionmulticontrols.com
E-mail: precisionmultiple@worldnet.att.net

Prescolite-Moldcast
Electrical & Lighting
1251 Doolittle Dr.
San Leandro, CA 94577
Phone: 510-562-3500
Fax: 510-577-5022

Preso-Matic Keyless Locks
Hardware
100-A Commerce Way
Sanford, FL 32771
Phone: 407-324-9933
Toll-free: 800-269-4234
Fax: 407-328-9977
E-mail: campbell@parkave.net

Price Pfister
Plumbing, Faucets & Fixtures
13500 Paxton St.
Pacoima, CA 91331
Phone: 818-896-1141
Toll-free: 800-PFAUCET
Fax: 818-686-4883
Internet: www.pricepfister.com

Prime-Line Products Co.
Doors—Exterior
5405 N. Industrial Pkwy.
San Bernardino, CA 92407
Phone: 909-887-8118
Fax: 909-880-8968
E-mail: dugl@prime-line-products.com

Pro Smart Inc.
Specialty Products
2741 West Oxford Ave.
No. 2
Englewood, CO 80110
Phone: 303-762-0700
Fax: 303-789-1223

Pro-Flo Products
Plumbing, Faucets & Fixtures
30 Commerce Rd.
Cedar Grove, NJ 07009
Phone: 973-239-2400
Toll-free: 800-325-1057
Fax: 973-239-5817

Progress Lighting
Electrical & Lighting
P.O. Box 5704
Spartanburg, SC 29304-5704
Phone: 864-599-6000
Fax: 864-599-6151
Internet: www.progresslighting.com
E-mail: rmueller@progresslighting.com

PSG Controls, Inc.
HVAC
1225 Tunnel Rd.
Perkasie, PA 18944
Phone: 215-257-3621
Toll-free: 800-782-8412
Fax: 215-257-4288

Q

Quality Woods
Flooring
95 Bartley Rd.
Flanders, NJ 07836
Phone: 973-584-7554
Toll-free: 800-637-6525
Fax: 973-584-3875

Quarry Tile Co.
Flooring
6328 E. Utah Ave.
Spokane, WA 99212
Phone: 509-536-2812
Toll-free: 800-423-2608
Fax: 509-536-4072
E-mail: quarrytile@hotmail.com

R

R & D Equipment
Doors—Exterior; Hardware; Landscaping & Outdoor Products
1150 Tri-View Ave.
Sioux City, IA 51103
Phone: 712-255-5205
Toll-free: 800-798-5678
Fax: 712-255-8292

Radiant Technology
HVAC
11A Farber Dr.
Bellport, NY 11713
Phone: 516-286-0900
Toll-free: 800-784-0234
Fax: 516-286-0947
Internet: www.radiant-tech.com
E-mail: radtech2@usa.pipeline.com

Rainsoft Water Treatment Systems
(A Div. of Aquion Partners)
Plumbing, Faucets & Fixtures
2080 E. Lunt Ave.
Elk Grove Village, IL 60007
Phone: 847-437-9400
Toll-free: 800-860-7638
Fax: 847-437-1594
Internet: www.aquion.com

Rapetti Faucets
(A Div. of George Blotcher)
Plumbing, Faucets & Fixtures
Zero High St.
Plainville, MA 02762
Phone: 508-699-9400
Toll-free: 800-688-5500
Fax: 508-699-9498

RAS Industries
Life-time Pre-formed Millwork
Structural Systems
12 Arentzen Blvd.
Charleroi, PA 15022
Phone: 412-489-1111
Toll-free: 800-367-1076
Fax: 800-367-8685
Internet: www.rasindustries.com

Raylux
Electrical & Lighting
P.O. Box 619
Nanuet, NY 10954-0619
Phone: 914-623-3471
Fax: 914-623-1861
Internet: www.ctr.be
E-mail: raylux@juno.com

Regency Industries
Plumbing, Faucets & Fixtures
27843 Peninsula Dr., S.
PO Box 5554
Blue Jay, CA 92321
Phone: 909-337-3752
Fax: 909-336-6744

Rehau
HVAC; Landscaping & Outdoor Products
P.O. Box 1706
Leesburg, VA 20177
Phone: 703-777-5255
Toll-free: 800-247-9445
Fax: 800-627-3428
Internet: www.rehau-na.com

Renato Specialty Products
Appliances
2775 W. Kingsley Rd.
Garland, TX 75040
Phone: 972-864-8800
Toll-free: 800-876-9731
Fax: 972-864-8900
Internet: www.renatos.com
E-mail: renatos@renatos.com

Republic Stainless Steel Sinks
Plumbing, Faucets & Fixtures
PO Box 1010
Ruston, LA 71273
Phone: 318-255-5600
Toll-free: 800-637-6485
Fax: 318-255-5653

Research Products
HVAC
P.O. Box 1467
Madison, WI 53701-1467
Phone: 608-257-8801
Fax: 608-257-4357
Internet: www.resprod.com

Rheem Mfg.
Air Conditioning Div.
HVAC
5600 Old Greenwood Rd.
Fort Smith, AR 72917-7010
Phone: 501-646-4311

Fax: 501-648-4918
Internet: www.rheemac.com

Richlund Enterprises
Appliances
608 Third St.
Kentwood, LA 70444
Phone: 504-229-4922
Fax: 504-229-4956
Internet: www.richlundsales.com

Rio Plastics
Structural Systems
PO Box 3707
Brownsville, TX 78523
Phone: 956-831-2715
Fax: 956-831-9851
Internet: www.rioplastics.com
E-mail: info@rioplastics.com

Robbins Hardwood Flooring
An Armstrong Company
Flooring
16803 Dallas Pkwy.
Addison, TX 75001
Phone: 214-887-2100
Toll-free: 800-733-3309
Fax: 214-887-2234
Internet: www.robbinsflooring.com

Robern
Electrical & Lighting; Walls, Finishes & Insulation
701 N. Wilson Ave.
Bristol, PA 19007
Phone: 215-826-9800
Toll-free: 800-877-2376
Fax: 215-826-9633
Internet: www.robern.com
E-mail: mark@robern.com

Roberts Step-Lite Systems
Electrical & Lighting; Landscaping & Outdoor Products
8413 Mantle Ave.
Oklahoma City, OK 73132
Phone: 405-728-4895
Fax: 405-728-4878

Rocktile Specialty Products
Countertops; Flooring
8814 W. Goose Creek Rd.
Boise, ID 83703
Phone: 208-342-7700
Toll-free: 800-545-7735
Fax: 208-342-7880

Rohl
Plumbing, Faucets & Fixtures
1559 Sunland
Costa Mesa, CA 92626
Phone: 714-557-1933
Toll-free: 800-777-9762
Fax: 714-557-8635
Internet: www.rohlhome.com
E-mail: info@rohlhome.com

Roto Frank of America
Windows & Glass
P.O. Box 599
Research Park
Chester, CT 06412-0599
Phone: 860-526-4996
Toll-free: 800-243-0893
Fax: 860-526-3785
E-mail: chester@roto-frank.com

Rynone Mfg. Corp.
Cabinetry; Countertops; Plumbing, Faucets & Fixtures
P.O. Box 128
N. Thomas Ave.
Sayre, PA 18840
Phone: 570-888-5272
Fax: 570-888-1175

S

SafeTek Intl.
Plumbing, Faucets & Fixtures; Specialty Products
1075 American Pacific Dr.
Henderson, NV 89014
Phone: 702-558-8202
Fax: 702-558-4535
Internet: www.safetekint.com
E-mail: j.fawcett@safetekint.com

Sandy Pond Hardwoods
Flooring
921-A Lancaster Pike
Quarryville, PA 17566
Phone: 717-284-5030
Toll-free: 800-546-9663
Fax: 717-284-5739
Internet: www.figuredhardwoods.com
E-mail: sph2prlg@ptdprolog.net

Satin Finish Hardwood Flooring
Flooring
8 Oak St.
Weston, ON M9N 1R8 Canada
Phone: 416-241-8651
Toll-free: 800-26SATIN
Fax: 416-241-8636

Screenex Retractable Door Systems Mfg.
Structural Systems; Windows & Glass
759 Zena Highwoods Rd.
Kingston, NY 12401
Phone: 914-246-3432
Toll-free: 800-746-7326
Fax: 800-RIORDAN
Internet: www.screenex.com
E-mail: screenex@aol.com

Sealeze
Doors—Exterior
8000 Whitepine Rd.
Richmond, VA 23237
Phone: 804-743-0982
Toll-free: 800-446-7325
Fax: 804-743-0051
E-mail: weatherseal@sealeze.com

Seating Innovations
Structural Systems; Windows & Glass
445 W. 1260 S.
Orem, UT 84057
Phone: 801-221-1110
Toll-free: 888-864-3463
Fax: 801-221-1262
Internet: www.seating-innovations.com

Sections, Inc.
Garage Doors, Openers & Accessories
1331 Larc Industrial Blvd.
Burnsville, MN 55337
Phone: 612-707-8810
Toll-free: 877-707-8810
Fax: 612-707-8809
Internet: www.sections.com
E-mail: jscott@sections.com

Selby Furniture Hardware Co.
Cabinetry
321 Rider Ave.
Bronx, NY 10451
Phone: 718-993-3700
Fax: 718-993-3143
Internet: www.selbyhardware.com
www.selbyexclusives.com
E-mail: selbern@aol.com

Semco Windows & Doors
Semling-Menke Co.
Doors—Exterior
P.O. Box 378
Merrill, WI 54452
Phone: 715-536-9411
Toll-free: 800-333-2206
Fax: 715-536-3067
Internet: www.semcowindows.com

SEPCO Industries
Plumbing, Faucets & Fixtures
491 Wortman Ave.
Spring Creek, NY 11208
Phone: 718-257-2800
Toll-free: 800-842-7277
Fax: 718-257-2144
Internet: www.sepcofaucets.com
E-mail: jabel@sepcofaucets.com

Sharp Electronics Corp.
Appliances
Sharp Plaza
Mahwah, NJ 07430
Phone: 201-529-8698
Toll-free: 800-BE-SHARP
Fax: 201-529-9597

Sibes Brass
Hardware
260 Lambert St., Ste. K
Oxnard, CA 93030
Phone: 805-988-0232
Toll-free: 800-483-4951
Fax: 805-988-9493
Internet: www.sibesbrass.com
E-mail: harvey@sibesbrass.com

SierraPine Ltd.
Cabinetry
2151 Professional Dr.
Suite 200
Roseville, CA 95661
Phone: 916-772-3422
Toll-free: 800-676-3339
Fax: 916-772-3419
Internet: www.sierrapine.com
E-mail: jlundegard@sierrapine.com

Sitecraft Inc.
Landscaping & Outdoor Products
40-25 Crescent St.
Long Island City, NY 11101
Phone: 800-221-1448
Toll-free: 800-221-1448
Fax: 718-729-4900
Internet: www.site-craft.com
E-mail: aseabra@rosenwachgroup.com

Slant/Fin Corp.
HVAC
100 Forest Dr.
Greenvale, NY 11548
Phone: 516-484-2600
Fax: 516-484-5921
Internet: www.slantfin.com

Smart Deck Systems
Landscaping & Outdoor Products
2600 W. Roosevelt Rd.
Chicago, IL 60608
Phone: 312-491-2500
Toll-free: 888-7DECKING
Fax: 312-491-2501
Internet: www.smartdeck.com

Smarthome.com
(A Home Automation Systems Co.)
Electrical & Lighting; Garage Doors, Openers & Accessories; Hardware; HVAC; Landscaping & Outdoor Products; Windows & Glass
17171 Daimler St.
Irvine, CA 92614
Phone: 949-221-9200
Toll-free: 800-762-7846
Fax: 949-221-9240
Internet: www.smarthome.com
E-mail: smarthome@smarthome.com

SmartLinc
Electrical & Lighting
17201 Daimler St.
Irvine, CA 92614
Phone: 949-221-0480
Toll-free: 888-540-9955
Fax: 949-221-0488
Internet: www.smartlinc.com
E-mail: inbox@smartlinc.com

SNOC
Landscaping & Outdoor Products
17200 Centrale
St-Hyacinthe, PQ J2T 4J7
Canada
Phone: 450-774-5238
Toll-free: 800-461-7662
Fax: 450-774-1954

Soft-Lite Windows
Windows & Glass
7009 Krick Rd.
Bedford, OH 44146
Phone: 440-232-9200
Fax: 440-232-7642
Internet: www.softlitewindows.com

SOLATUBE Intl.
Electrical & Lighting
2210 Oak Ridge Way
Vista, CA 92083
Phone: 760-597-4400
Toll-free: 800-773-SOLA
Fax: 760-599-5181
Internet: www.solatube.com

Solnhofen Natural Stone
Flooring
1604 17th St.
San Francisco, CA 94107
Phone: 415-552-1500
Fax: 415-552-3500
Internet: www.solnhofen.com
E-mail: solnhofen@earthlink.com

Southland Spa & Sauna
Landscaping & Outdoor Products; Plumbing, Faucets & Fixtures
P.O. Box 638
Ray Farm Rd.
Haleyville, AL 35565
Phone: 205-486-7919
Fax: 205-486-7793
E-mail: southspa@sonett.net

Space-Metrics
Specialty Products
885 Market St.
Oregon, WI 53575
Phone: 608-835-8850
Fax: 608-835-8860

Space-Ray Infrared Gas Heaters
HVAC
305 Dogget St.
P.O. Box 36485
Charlotte, NC 28236
Phone: 704-372-3485
Toll-free: 800-438-4936
Fax: 704-332-5843

Speakman Co.
Mfg. Div.
Plumbing, Faucets & Fixtures
PO Box 191
Wilmington, DE 19899-0191
Phone: 302-764-9100
Toll-free: 800-537-2107
Fax: 800-977-2747
Internet: www.speakmancompany.com
E-mail: jfleitz@speakmancompany.com

Specialty Lighting
Electrical & Lighting
639 Washburn Switch Rd.
Shelby, NC 28151
Phone: 704-482-3416
Fax: 704-484-0818

Spruce Environmental Technologies
HVAC
187 Neck Rd.
P.O. Box 8244
Ward Hill, MA 01835
Phone: 978-521-0901
Toll-free: 800-355-0901
Fax: 978-521-3964
Internet: www.spruce.com
E-mail: sales@spruce.com

SSHC, Inc.
HVAC
146 Elm St., Box 769
Old Saybrook, CT 06475
Phone: 860-388-3848
Toll-free: 800-544-5182
Fax: 860-388-0525
Internet: www.sshcinc.com
E-mail: info@sshcinc.com

St. Thomas Classics
(A Div. of St. Thomas Creations)
Plumbing, Faucets & Fixtures
1022 W. 24th St., Ste. 125
National City, CA 91950-6302
Phone: 619-474-9490
Toll-free: 800-536-2284
Fax: 619-474-9493
Internet: www.stthomascreations.com
E-mail: stthomas@stthomascreations.com

St. Thomas Creations
Plumbing, Faucets & Fixtures
1022 W. 24th St., Ste. 125
National City, CA 91950-6302
Phone: 619-474-9490
Toll-free: 800-536-2284
Fax: 619-474-9493
Internet: www.stthomascreations.com

Starfire Lighting
Electrical & Lighting
317 St. Pauls Ave.
Jersey City, NJ 07306
Toll-free: 800-443-8823
Fax: 201-656-0666

Steelwood Doors
A Member of the Royal Group of Companies
Doors—Exterior
239 Chrislea Rd.
Woodbridge, ON L4L 8N4
Canada
Phone: 905-851-4665
Fax: 905-851-7340

Sterling Plumbing Group
Plumbing, Faucets & Fixtures
2900 Golf Rd.
Rolling Meadows, IL 60008
Phone: 847-734-1777
Toll-free: 800-STERLING
Fax: 847-734-4767
Internet: www.sterlingplumbing.com

Strom Plumbing By Sign Of The Crab
Hardware; Plumbing, Faucets & Fixtures
Dept. RM, 3756 Omec Cir.
Rancho Cordova, CA 95742-7399
Phone: 916-638-2722
Toll-free: 800-843-2722
Fax: 916-638-2725
Internet: www.signofthecrab.com

The Structural Slate Co.
Countertops; Flooring
222 E. Main St.
Pen Argyl, PA 18072
Phone: 610-863-4141
Toll-free: 800-677-5283
Fax: 610-863-7016
Internet: www.structuralslate@ptd.net
E-mail: ssco1@ptd.net

Sub-Zero Freezer Co.
Appliances
4717 Hammersley Rd.
Madison, WI 53711
Phone: 608-271-2233
Toll-free: 800-222-7820
Fax: 608-270-3339
Internet: www.subzero.com

Summitville Tiles
Countertops; Flooring
P.O. Box 73
Summitville, OH 43962
Phone: 330-223-1511
Fax: 330-223-1414
Internet: www.summitville.com

Sun Room Designs, Inc.
Structural Systems; Windows & Glass
Depot & First Sts.
Youngwood, PA 15697
Phone: 724-925-1100
Toll-free: 800-621-1110
Fax: 724-925-9172
Internet: www.sunroomdesigns.com
E-mail: sunroom@trib.infi.net

Sun Tunnel Skylights
Electrical & Lighting, HVAC
786 McGlincey Ln.
Campbell, CA 95008
Phone: 408-369-7447
Toll-free: 800-369-3664
Fax: 408-369-0228
Internet: www.suntunnel.com
E-mail: sun2000@netcom.industry.net

SunPorch Structures
Structural Systems
495 Post Rd. E.
Westport, CT 06880-4400
Phone: 203-454-0040
Toll-free: 800-221-2550
Fax: 203-454-0020

Manufacturers & Suppliers Index

SunStar Heating Products
HVAC
P.O. Box 36271
Charlotte, NC 28236-6271
Phone: 704-372-3486
Toll-free: 888-778-6782
Fax: 704-332-5843
Internet: www.
sunstarheaters.com
E-mail: info@
sunstarheaters.com

Superior Fireplace Co.
Specialty Products
4325 Artesia Ave.
Fullerton, CA 92633
Phone: 714-521-7302
Toll-free: 800-731-8101
Fax: 714-521-5223
Internet: www.
superiorfireplace.com

Sure-Lites
(A Brand of Cooper Lighting)
Electrical & Lighting
400 Busse Rd.
Elk Grove Village, IL 60007
Phone: 847-956-8400
Fax: 847-956-1537
Internet: www.cooperlighting.
com

Swivelier
Electrical & Lighting
P.O. Box 619
Nanuet, NY 10954-0619
Phone: 914-623-3471
Fax: 914-623-1861
E-mail: swivelier@juno.com

Symmons Industries
Plumbing, Faucets & Fixtures
31 Brooks Dr.
Braintree, MA 02184-3804
Phone: 781-848-2250
Toll-free: 800-SYMMONS
Fax: 781-961-9621
Internet: www.symmons.com

Systematic Irrigation Controls
Landscaping & Outdoor Products; Plumbing, Faucets & Fixtures
P.O. Box 8051
Newport Beach, CA 92660
Phone: 949-347-1922
Toll-free: 800-597-2835
Fax: 949-347-1941
E-mail: envsystm@aol.com

T

Targetti USA
Electrical & Lighting
1513 East St. Gertrude Place
Santa Ana, CA 92705
Phone: 714-708-8765
Toll-free: 888-578-8111
Fax: 714-595-9924

Temco Fireplace Products
Specialty Products
301 S. Perimeter Park Dr.
Ste. 227
Nashville, TN 37211
Phone: 615-831-9393
Fax: 615-831-9127
Internet: www.
temcofireplaces.com
E-mail: temco@
compuserve.com

Terra-Green Ceramics
Flooring
1650 Progress Dr.
Richmond, IN 47374
Phone: 765-935-4760
Fax: 765-935-3971
Internet: www.
terragreenceramics.com

Texas Woods, Inc.
Flooring; Landscaping & Outdoor Products
Rt. 1 Box 66
Bastrop, TX 78602
Phone: 512-321-7000
Toll-free: 800-687-1779
Fax: 512-303-7700
Internet: www.texaswoods.com
E-mail: mesquite@bastrop.com

TFI Corp.
Avanté
Plumbing, Faucets & Fixtures
2812 Hegan Ln.
Chico, CA 95928
Phone: 530-891-6390
Toll-free: 800-752-2037
Fax: 530-893-1273
Internet: www.tficorp.com

Thermoplast
Windows & Glass
3035 Blvd. le Corbusier
Laval, PQ H7L 4C3 Canada
Phone: 450-687-5115
Toll-free: 800-361-9261
Fax: 450-687-5196
Internet: www.thermoplast.com

Thermo-Vu Sunlite Industries
Walls, Finishes & Insulation; Windows & Glass
51 Rodeo Dr.
Brentwood, NY 11717
Phone: 516-243-1000
Toll-free: 800-883-5483
Fax: 516-243-1004
Internet: www.thermo-vu.com
E-mail: sales@thermo-vu.com

Thomas Lighting
Consumer Div.
Electrical & Lighting; Landscaping & Outdoor Products
950 Breckinridge Ln.
Ste. G50
Louisville, KY 40207
Phone: 502-894-2400
Toll-free: 800-36LIGHT
Fax: 502-894-2427
Internet: www.thomaslighting.
com

Timber Tech
Landscaping & Outdoor Products
2141 Fairwood Ave.
Colombus, OH 43207
Phone: 614-443-7697
Toll-free: 800-307-7780
Fax: 614-443-7698
Internet: www.timbertech.com

TIR Systems Ltd.
Landscaping & Outdoor Products
3350 Bridgeway St.
Vancouver, BC V5K 1H9
Canada
Phone: 604-294-8477
Toll-free: 800-663-2036
Fax: 604-294-3733
Internet: www.tirsys.com

Titon Inc.
HVAC
P.O. Box 6164
South Bend, IN 46660
Phone: 219-271-9699
Fax: 219-271-9771
Internet: www.titon.com
E-mail: titoninc@aol.com

Tivoli Industries
Electrical & Lighting
1513 East St. Gertrude Pl.
Santa Ana, CA 92705
Phone: 800-854-3288
Fax: 714-957-1501

Tork
Electrical & Lighting
1 Grove
Mount Vernon, NY 10550
Phone: 914-664-3542
Fax: 914-664-5052

Toto USA
Plumbing, Faucets & Fixtures
1155 Southern Rd.
Morrow, GA 30260
Toll-free: 800-350-8686
Fax: 770-282-8701
Internet: www.totousa.com

Trex Company
Landscaping & Outdoor Products
20 S. Cameron St.
Winchester, VA 22601
Phone: 540-678-4070
Toll-free: 800-BUY-TREX
Fax: 540-678-1820
Internet: www.trex.com
E-mail: marketing@trex.com

Tri-Guards
Doors—Interior; Walls, Finishes & Insulation
490 Hintz Rd.
Wheeling, IL 60090
Phone: 847-451-8444
Toll-free: 800-783-8445
Fax: 847-537-8507

Truth Hardware
Hardware; Windows & Glass
700 W. Bridge St.
Owatonna, MN 55060
Phone: 507-451-5620
Toll-free: 800-866-7884
Fax: 507-451-5655
Internet: www.truth.com
E-mail: truthsal@truth.com

Tubular Skylighte, Inc.
Electrical & Lighting
753 Cattlemen Rd.
Sarasota, FL 34232
Phone: 941-378-TUBE
Toll-free: 800-315-TUBE
Fax: 941-342-8844
Internet: www.
tubular-skylight.com
E-mail: sales@tubular-skylight.
com

U

UniBoard Canada
(St-Laurent Div.)
Flooring
5605 Cypihot St.
Saint-Laurent, PQ H4S 1R3
Canada
Phone: 514-335-2003
Toll-free: 800-361-7502
Fax: 514-335-7763

Uni-Group U.S.A.
Manufacturers of Uni
Concrete Pavers
Landscaping & Outdoor Products
4362 Northlake Blvd.
Suite 207
Palm Beach Gardens, FL 33410
Phone: 561-626-4666
Toll-free: 800-872-1864
Fax: 561-627-6403
Internet: www.
uni-groupusa.org
E-mail: info@uni-groupusa.org

United States Ceramic Tile Co.
Countertops; Flooring
10233 Sandyville Rd., S.E.
East Sparta, OH 44626-9333
Phone: 330-866-5531
Toll-free: 800-321-0684
Fax: 330-866-5340
Internet: www.
usceramictileco.com

Universal Marble & Granite
Countertops; Flooring
1919 Halethorpe Farms Rd.
Baltimore, MD 21227
Phone: 410-247-2442
Toll-free: 800-828-5611
Fax: 410-247-8043

V

VACUFLO—H-P Products
Specialty Products
512 W. Gorgas St.
Louisville, OH 44641
Phone: 330-875-5556
Toll-free: 800-822-8356
Fax: 330-875-7584
Internet: www.vacuflo.com
E-mail: vacuflo@hpproducts.net

Vance Industries
Cabinetry; Specialty Products
250 Wille Rd.
Des Plaines, IL 60018
Phone: 847-375-8900
Fax: 847-375-6818

Vanguard Industries
HVAC
831 N. Vanguard St.
McPherson, KS 67460
Phone: 316-241-6369
Toll-free: 800-775-5039

Fax: 316-241-1772
Internet: www.
vanguardpipe.com
E-mail: service@
vanguardpipe.com

Vanguard Plastics Ltd.
Specialty Products
19239 96th Ave.
Surrey, BC V4N 4C4 Canada
Phone: 604-888-2511
Toll-free: 800-663-0077
Fax: 604-888-5330
Internet: www.
vanguard-plastics.com
E-mail: support@
vanguard-plastics.com

Vent-A-Hood
Specialty Products
P.O. Box 830426
Richardson, TX 75083-0426
Phone: 972-235-5201
Internet: www.ventahood.com
E-mail: egober@ventahood.com

Vermont Castings
Specialty Products
1000 E. Market St.
Huntington, IN 46750
Phone: 219-356-8000
Toll-free: 800-227-8683
Internet: www.vermontcastings.
com

Vermont Marble Co.
Countertops; Flooring; Landscaping & Outdoor Products
52 Main St.
Proctor, VT 05765
Phone: 802-459-2300
Toll-free: 800-427-1396
Fax: 802-459-2948

Victor Sun Control
Windows & Glass
4101 G St.
Philadelphia, PA 19124
Phone: 215-743-0800
Fax: 215-743-3164
Internet: www.victorsun.com
E-mail: info@victorsun.com

Viking Range Corp.
Appliances
111 Front St.
P.O. Drawer 956
Greenwood, MS 38930
Phone: 662-455-1200
Toll-free: 888-845-4641
Fax: 662-453-7939
Internet: www.vikingrange.com

Vita Bath
Plumbing, Faucets & Fixtures
2320 N.W. 147th St.
Opa Locka, FL 33054
Phone: 305-685-5739
Toll-free: 800-848-2772
Fax: 305-688-9415
Internet: www.vitabathandspa.
com

W

Walker & Zanger
Countertops; Flooring; Landscaping & Outdoor Products
31 Warren Pl.
Mt. Vernon, NY 10550
Phone: 914-667-1600
Fax: 914-667-6244
Internet: www.
marblestone.com
E-mail: wzny@marblestone.com

Watercolors
Hardware; Plumbing, Faucets & Fixtures
Garrison, NY 10524
Phone: 914-424-3327
Fax: 914-424-3169

Watertech
Plumbing, Faucets & Fixtures
2507 Plymouth Rd.
Johnson City, TN 37601
Toll-free: 800-BUY-TUBS
Fax: 615-926-1470

Product Index

Product Index